Communication

Skills

HANDBOOK

REVISED AND UPDATED EDITION

Communication
Skills
HANDBOOK

How to succeed in written and oral communication

JANE SUMMERS

BRETT SMITH

WILEY
John Wiley & Sons Australia, Ltd

Revised and updated edition published 2004 by
John Wiley & Sons Australia, Ltd
33 Park Road, Milton, Qld 4064

Offices also in Sydney and Melbourne

First published 1995 by the Faculty of Business & Commerce,
The University of Southern Queensland
Second edition 1997
Third edition 2001
Fourth edition 2001
Fifth edition published 2002 by John Wiley & Sons Australia, Ltd
Revised 2003

National Library of Australia
Cataloguing-in-Publication data

Communication skills handbook: how to succeed in written and oral
communication.

   Rev. and updated ed.
   Bibliography.
   Includes index.
   For tertiary students.
   ISBN 0 470 80551 X.

   1. Written communication. 2. Oral communication.
   3. Communication in management. 1. Smith, Brett. II. Summers,
Jane.

658.45

Cover images: © 2001 PhotoDisc, Inc.

Printed in Singapore by
Craft Print International Ltd

10 9 8 7 6 5 4 3 2 1

Contents

Preface

This handbook is designed to assist university students at all levels to prepare and present written and verbal material. It does not claim to be comprehensive, but rather attempts to deal with the major problems students are likely to encounter in the preparation and presentation of work for assessment. The handbook also aims to minimise potential problems of inconsistency in requirements among different departments, faculties and universities. By outlining a series of standard expectations and formats for written and verbal material in Australian universities, we hope to alleviate some of the confusion expressed by many students.

Although this book attempts to provide an overview of generally accepted standards in terms of communication and presentation of assessable work, there will inevitably be minor variations between the guidelines presented here and the particular requirements for courses of study. Students are therefore strongly advised to consult their individual instructors for any specific guidelines they may require. Where no advice on formatting or style is available, we suggest that students use the information presented in the following pages.

For more detailed guidance on preparing and presenting written reports and assignments, the Commonwealth Government's *Style manual* (2002, now in its sixth edition) has long been regarded as the standard work of reference for all authors, editors and printers in Australia. To assist students, a quick reference guide to the *Style manual* is included in Chapter 1.

This handbook has received overwhelming endorsement from both students and staff since its inception in 1995. Amendments and improvements are constantly being made to ensure that it remains current while maintaining its brevity and relevance. To this end, we are always grateful for feedback from university students or staff.

Jane Summers
Brett Smith
September 2003

Objectives

The objectives of this handbook are:

- to provide students with guidelines that are consistent across their university studies and to outline the minimum requirements for formal presentation of written and verbal assignments

- to assist university staff to apply a consistent approach to the assessment of formally presented written and verbal material by students, irrespective of university, department, course or level of study

- to reinforce among students the view that communication skills are an integral component of their studies and essential to their careers, rather than optional skills isolated from their chosen disciplines.

Explanation of symbols

The following symbols are used throughout this book to highlight features that have proved particularly useful for students:

     Hints

     Examples of concepts being discussed

Acknowledgements

This handbook uses recommendations and examples from a range of sources. In particular, we acknowledge the input and advice from the staff of the Faculties of Business, Commerce and Arts at the University of Southern Queensland and, for guides to layout and content, the Business Studies Department of the University of Queensland, Gatton College. Original conceptual ideas for this style of book for use by university students came from the work of Dr Jane Summers and Mr Cec Pederson while at Gatton College in 1993. Additional material and examples have been drawn from the sources listed in the List of References. The authors would also like to thank Rae Wear and Tricia Rooney for their valuable contributions to the creation and publication of the first edition of this book.

The following individuals also deserve mention for their specific contributions to this edition: Cec Pedersen, for his input into the sections on case studies and report writing; Dr Lesley Willcoxon for her help with the referencing section; Professor Chad Perry for his contribution to the section on thesis writing and for other general style comments; Frank Jarvis for his input into the examination techniques section; and Dr Meredith Lawley for her contributions to the general guidelines section.

General guidelines for assessment

1 General guidelines for assessment

1.1 Introduction

When preparing and presenting written material there are a number of key areas that, if addressed conscientiously, will help both to make the process easier and to increase the chances of achieving a satisfactory mark. The following points are universally accepted as applying to all written work, including assignments, reports, case studies, essays, books and journal articles.

Writing for assessment or review is a means of communicating ideas and/or demonstrating analytical skills in a structured way. Generally, the purpose of a written assignment is to inform the readers, to persuade them to consider a point of view, and possibly to solve a problem or provide recommendations for future action. It is *not* an opportunity for free-form self-expression.

1.2 Assignment preparation guidelines

Writing for assessment can be daunting, and students may be tempted to procrastinate, believing they can complete a satisfactory product the night before the due date. Such last-minute efforts are obvious to any marker. The following hints may prove helpful in making writing a less arduous task.

If you have a choice of topic for your assignments, be sure to choose an issue that appeals to your imagination and interest. This will make any research or study much easier.

 Try to find out *exactly* what the instructor is looking for:

1. Read and re-read the assignment information carefully and thoughtfully.

2. Read all guidance and instructions you are given relating to the assignment.

3. Listen to any audiotape instructions provided.

4. Share your views with other students in study groups, tutorial groups or electronic discussion groups where these are available.

5. If you remain uncertain, consult the instructor as a last resort.

It is important to continue to recheck the direction and focus of your work during the preparation and writing stages. Most courses will have very detailed assessment requirements, which may include marking guides or hints to help identify the correct focus or important points.

In general, markers will seek to determine whether you have:

- fully comprehended the point at issue and have kept to the topic
- argued the ideas within the word limits (if provided)
- presented your thoughts reflectively and critically (marks will generally be lost for unsupported opinion)
- shown an original and imaginative approach to the topic
- shown evidence of extensive reading and research on the topic or issue (demonstrated through in-text referencing and a list of references)
- presented your thoughts coherently and logically.

Make sure that you have clearly understood the question, and check that all required components have been addressed. For example, does the question contain a descriptive or analytical element, or an element requiring your opinion and suggestions? It is possible that the assignment will contain a number of different elements. (Refer to the glossary on page 93 for definitions of directive terms.)

Writing assignments needs planning in order to ensure that all relevant elements have been addressed and that the finished material is presented in a logical manner (i.e. after a suitable introduction, one idea leads to the next and finally to the conclusion). Where appropriate, make use of minor headings to assist in structuring and focusing your work. Headings help the reader follow your argument. In assignments that include headings, consider using a side heading every two or three pages and a run-in heading (set in bold, and ending with a full stop, at the start of the first line of text) every three or four paragraphs. Running heads may also sometimes be useful.

Good academic writing requires not only carefully structured analysis but also a thoughtful balancing of theoretical ideas and their application to the topic. Analysis is not purely descriptive; theory should be used as a framework to support your arguments and conclusions.

1.3 Writing guidelines

It is important to remember not to write in the same way that you speak. Conversational English is not acceptable in any formal or assessable writing. A formal style should be adopted, and the use of colloquialisms or slang words and phrases, which might be acceptable in conversation, should be avoided (see Figure 1.1 for examples).

The reason for this is that written work, unlike the spoken word, is a permanent transcript of a writer's thoughts and ideas. The reader has time to go back over what was said and to consider the way information has been presented.

In a conversation or oral presentation there is an opportunity for immediate clarification of points that are unclear. In written work this is not possible. The reader must interpret your meaning and conclusions as you have presented them, without the benefit of explanation or clarification from you, the writer. Therefore, you must choose your words carefully and provide the reader with a logical progression of thoughts and evidence that leads to the conclusion. To this end, the following points should be considered:

- Ensure the work is completed at least one day before the due date (preferably longer) to allow time for proofreading. It is often useful to give the work to someone not involved with the subject to read. If that person understands it and agrees with your conclusion, it is likely that you have produced a well-structured piece of writing. If this option is not possible, many writers find it valuable to read the report aloud (make sure no one else is around!). This helps you determine what you have really written (not what you **meant** to say) and helps to establish the natural punctuation breaks and emphases (see Figure 1.1 for more hints and examples of common errors in punctuation and grammar).

- Checking spelling has been made much easier by word processing software. If you are using a computer to prepare an assignment, then you should use the spellcheck function before submitting the assignment. This will not, however, pick up words that have been misused. Words often confused by students include *its* and *it's*; *affect* and *effect*; *compliment* and *complement*; *alternate* and *alternative*. There are many guides to English usage that can help. If you are not using a computerised spellchecker, a dictionary must be used to ensure no errors in spelling have occurred.

- Care must be taken to ensure that all work is free of spelling, grammatical and punctuation errors. It is inexcusable for any assessable written work to feature any of these problems.

- Slang and conversational English should be avoided (see Figure 1.1).

- Be sparing in the use of adjectives and adverbs, which often are essentially value judgements.

- Many style guides recommend against the use of contractions (e.g. *don't*, *can't*, *haven't*) in formal writing. This recommendation applies to assignment submissions, too.

- Some contractions and abbreviations do have a place in academic assignments. For example, in reference citations you may use such contractions as eds (for editors), edn (edition) and nos (numbers), and abbreviations such as vol. (for volume), pers. comm. (personal communication), ver. (version), rev. (revised), n.d. (no date). Be careful to distinguish between contractions, which include the last letter of the word and so do not take a full stop, and abbreviations, which end with a full stop to denote omitted letters at the end of the word. Established abbreviations such as 'US' (used only as an adjective) and 'ASEAN' do not require full stops.

- Use italics for emphasis very sparingly (as a rule of thumb, no more than once or twice per page). Overuse of italics reduces its impact.

- Use single quotation marks, except for quotes within quotes, for which double quotation marks should be used.

- Capital letters are used for the first letter in every sentence, the pronoun 'I' and the initial letter of all proper names (i.e. the names of people, places, organisations, book titles and so on). Initial capitals should be used for a full or specific title, but lower case should be used otherwise. For example, 'The University of Southern Queensland was one of many universities visited by Prime Minister Howard. It has been rare for prime ministers in recent years to visit regional centres . . .' As a general rule of thumb, if in doubt, use lower case. Also, avoid using all capitals in headings; a mix of upper- and lower-case letters is easier to read.

- Formal work should be written in the third person, using plural pronouns (e.g. use *they* instead of *he* or *she*). This will ensure that all work is perceived as objective (not a personal, unsubstantiated view) and non-sexist. Occasional use of 'I' and 'we' is acceptable when describing what you actually did, but not to present your own value judgements (as in 'I feel . . .' or 'I consider . . .'). In report writing and case study analysis particularly, avoid using words like *I*, *me*, *we*, *our*, *he*, *she*. Refer to the *Style manual* (Commonwealth of Australia 2002, pp. 55–62) for more information.

1.3.1 Non-offensive language

Be careful to avoid using discriminatory language. As the *Style manual* puts it:

> Linguistic discrimination can take various forms that may marginalise or exclude particular segments of the population — whether unwittingly or not. Stereotypical description of any group of people or a member of an identifiable group is probably the most insidious . . . When referring to an individual, that person's sex, religion, nationality, racial group, age or physical or mental characteristics should only be mentioned if this information is pertinent to the discussion. (p. 55)

Writers should always pay particular attention to context — all writing has a context — and should be guided by discretion, tact and sensitivity in making the necessary decisions on appropriate language. Furthermore, they:

> should always bear in mind the diversity within their audiences, and ensure that references to and about particular people or social groups are couched in inclusive terms. (p. 55)

Read the *Style manual* (2002, pp. 55–62) for further guidance.

1.3.2 Use of numbers

Numbers should be expressed in figures when they accompany a symbol or unit of measurement and in tables. For example, *$6.50, 9.45 am, 60 L, 9%* and *16 years*.

When showing statistical results using percentages, the word *percent* must be written out, except in a table, where the percentage symbol (%) should be used.

When using numbers, the Australian standard is to use a space to separate each group of three figures in numbers greater than 999. For example, *5 000*, *10 000* and *2 000 000*. Commas are not recommended to separate large numbers.

If presenting numbers smaller than unity, a zero should be placed before the decimal point. For example, *0.25* and *0.67*.

Numbers below 100 are generally expressed in words; however, numbers greater than ninety-nine may also be expressed in words when the numerical expressions are used to convey approximation.

Only a few hundred people attended the game, in spite of the 800 flyers distributed to people in the area.

Numbers that begin a sentence should be expressed in words; this also applies to years.

Nineteen ninety-four will always be remembered ...

If using two series of numbers in a passage, one series should be expressed as words and the other as numbers to avoid confusion.

Twelve students scored 16 marks, and thirty students scored 24 marks.

Use numerals for parts of a document (e.g. 'Chapter 3' or 'Figure 6.4').

If a number includes a fraction or refers to a page number, or if there are sets of numerals, some of which are higher than ten, they should all be expressed as a number. For example, *7, 21, 133*, not *seven, 21, 133*. Dates are written as *23 April 2001*; decades as *the 1970s* (not *the 1970's*); year spans as *1984–85* (not *1984–5*).

1.3.3 Tables, figures and graphs

Tables, which are generally systematic presentations of data in columns and rows, are used to clarify complicated data. Note that an examiner should not *have* to look at tables and figures in order to follow your argument. Any important points made in a table or figure should be incorporated in your text. Similarly, tables and figures should be comprehensible, independent of the text, so titles and column and row headings should be self-explanatory.

Figures are used to represent information such as models diagrammatically in line drawings, pictures and other illustrative forms. They can also be used to present textual information that cannot be shown logically in tabular form (i.e. in columns and rows).

All tables, figures and graphs used in your assignments must:

■ have a clearly definable purpose and be referred to in the body of your work

■ have a caption or title set in bold

- be numbered, and be referred to in the text by that number rather than by 'above' or 'below'

- be enclosed by a border or in a box

- be referenced correctly when referring to another author's work, noting if adaptations have been made to the original work (see Section 2.3 for referencing techniques). A source line beneath a table or figure will normally be in italic (e.g. *Source: Gibbs (1999, p. 63)*).

Table, figure and graph numbering should follow paragraph numbering; that is, in Chapter 2 of the document, all tables would be numbered *2.1, 2.2, 2.3* etc. in sequential order. The same principle applies to graphs and figures.

Figure and table titles should be clearly descriptive and 0.5 to 0.75 of a line long.

1.3.4 Titles

The title you choose for your work, whether a report, a case study, an essay or an oral presentation, is important, as it provides the reader with a first impression and can either stimulate interest or extinguish it! Consider the following title:

'A study of how expenditure patterns of persons 55 years and above vary with time using a longitudinal survey consisting of household expenditure diaries distributed to a random sample of households in urban Queensland.'

It is certainly informative, but it is also far too long. Ideally, you should aim for a title of about eight words. Here are some alternatives to the above:

'Expenditure of the aged' (too short and uninformative)

'A conceptualisation of a theoretical exemplar for an analysis of deviant aged expenditure' (too much jargon)

'The effect of life stage on expenditure patterns for the aged'

'A model for analysing different levels of expenditure for the aged'

The last two titles are both clearly expressed and about the right length. The appropriate choice may depend on the line of argument the writer has chosen. In some assessments you will need to write the question or essay statement as your title.

1.3.5 Foreign terms and acronyms

Foreign terms that have not been fully absorbed into everyday English are written in italics. This does not apply to foreign terms in common use, such as laissez faire or ad hoc. If in doubt, consult a dictionary.

The first time they are used, acronyms or abbreviations should be placed in parentheses after the full name. Later references need simply use the abbreviation.

The Electoral and Administrative Review Commission (EARC) indicated in its report that ... Nevertheless, EARC went on to recommend ...

1.3.6 Parentheses

Parentheses are used to enclose expressions that are not essential to the meaning of the sentence but that amplify or clarify it, or offer an aside.

 There were many at the trial who believed that Smith behaved unfairly (or so they said), whereas the outcome did not reflect this view.

Parentheses are also used to enclose letters or numbers designating a series either at the beginning of a paragraph or within a sentence, as in *(a)*, *(b)* and *(c)* or *(i)*, *(ii)* and *(iii)*, and so on.

Parentheses are also used to enclose in-text reference (author–date) information.

 It is well known that whales move along the Queensland coast during the winter months to reach their breeding grounds (Smith 1999).

The punctuation used with parentheses is governed by the grammatical demands of the enclosed expression; that is, if the statement in parentheses requires a full stop, question mark or exclamation mark, then these should appear within the parentheses. A comma should be used after the parentheses only if it would have been required if the parenthetical element was not there.

 The topic of his thesis (Are men really from Mars?) was controversial.

Loud applause greeted the cast (all members of the final-year student body), with the result that many felt quite emotional about the performance.

Some of the buildings that the students were studying in their architecture course had very mixed styles. (It is worth noting that this particular region is well known for the diverse mixture of architectural styles.)

Square brackets are used to enclose words or phrases inserted in quoted text by someone other than the author of the quotation.

 He writes in his biography, 'Although I grew up in Darwin, I was born in Toowoomba [a large inland city two hours north of Brisbane], where my father ran a local store.'

Square brackets are also used to denote other interpolations, such as *[continued overleaf]* or *[turn to p. 44]*.

1.3.7 Points of ellipsis

The principal use of the three points of ellipsis (...) is to mark the omission of words within a quoted passage.

 Every student ... must, before submitting his or her assignment, sign the declaration of original work ...

Note that only three points are used even if the ellipsis comes at the end of a sentence. No punctuation mark should precede the first point or follow the last point. It is important to use marks of ellipsis when your direct quotations omit parts of the text from which you are quoting. These points indicate to the reader that the material you have quoted has been shortened for the purpose of your writing.

In creative writing, ellipses are also used to indicate faltering speech or to suggest diffidence, reluctance or irony. For example:

But ... but ... I'm sure I did it!

This is the letter I spoke about a few weeks ago ...

Most of your assignment writing will use ellipses only in the former way, although for some of you who are writing up transcripts of interviews, for example, the latter situation may apply.

1.3.8 Bullet points

Use bullet points (sometimes called 'dot points') sparingly in academic writing, and only when the material in each point can be expressed as a phrase or clause ending with a semicolon or comma; that is, full sentences should not be used in bullet points. Do not indent a list of bullet points, and do not leave a blank line after the introduction to the list.

Table 1.1 presents a quick guide to useful and frequently referred to pages of the *Style manual* (2002).

TABLE 1.1 Quick reference to the *Style manual*	
TOPIC	**PAGE NO.**
Bulleted lists	141–4
Contractions and abbreviations	151–61
Dates	170–1
Foreign words and phrases	148–9
Harvard referencing style	188–208
Headings	137–40
Hyphens and prefixes	88–94
Inclusive communication	55–61
Names, titles and capital letters	119–35
Numbers	163–77
Points of ellipsis	110
Possessive apostrophe	85–7
Quotations	100, 113–16
Tables	346–58

Slang — to be avoided

'The experiment was a *dud.*' Not everyone knows what a 'dud' is.

'Sales *went through the roof.*' Not a very professional or informative way to say that sales increased rapidly.

Grammar/style — common errors

'It was done *so as* to prove the final result.' The '*so as*' is not needed in this sentence. Avoid unnecessary words.

'It was *obvious* that …' If it is obvious, you should not have to say it.

'*As said before*, the company was …' If it has been said before, do not repeat it; alternatively, think of another way of re-emphasising the point.

Punctuation — some hints

An apostrophe 's' can mean a noun becomes possessive; that is, something belongs to it. In cases where the noun ends in any letter other than an 's' or 'x', an apostrophe followed by an 's' signifies possession (e.g. 'John's leg hurt'; 'Kenwood's deep fryers were the most expensive').

If a noun already ends in an 's' or 'x' and is of one syllable, then possession is again indicated by an apostrophe 's' (e.g. 'Keats's poems', 'Marx's theories'). Exceptions to this rule include Classical names (e.g. 'Mars' wrath'). In words of more than one syllable ending in an 's' or 'x', only an apostrophe is added (e.g. 'Hopkins' poems').

An apostrophe can also indicate that a letter or letters are missing from the word or that two words have been combined to make a shorter one (a contraction) — *do not* becomes *don't* (the second 'o' is removed); *have not* becomes *haven't*, and so on.

A common mistake with the apostrophe is failing to distinguish between *its* and *it's*. Remember,

> *its* is possessive ('The dog loved its bone.')

> *it's* means 'it is' (the second 'i' is missing) ('It's a great day.')

FIGURE 1.1 Some common writing errors and hints

1.4 Presentation guidelines

When presenting written work, in addition to layout (discussed in Chapters 3, 4 and 5), adhering to a number of formatting requirements will help to make your work both easier to read and easier for the marker to grade. These requirements are outlined below.

- Leave a margin on all four edges of each page. Most word processing programs are set up with 2.5 cm top and bottom margins and 3.2 cm left and right margins. Check the requirements of your university.

- The preferred font size for most submissions is 12 point. Use a proportional font such as Times New Roman.

- Avoid using all upper-case type in text. Long passages set in upper case are difficult to read.

- Do not use bold to emphasise or highlight words or points; instead, underline the relevant words.

- Assignments must be typed — not hand-written — using $1\frac{1}{2}$-line spacing (unless otherwise specified). Executive summaries and lists of references should be set in single spacing. Leave a line space (blank line) between paragraphs and two line spaces between sections.

- Assignments should be submitted on A4 size paper, and only one side of each page should be used.

- Pages should be numbered in a consistent place on the page (e.g. at the top right or bottom centre of each page).

- Each new section or subsection need not commence on a new page. However, all major headings and subheadings should be clearly identified and numbered. Make sure that headings are not left by themselves at the bottom of pages. There should be at least two lines of text under a heading at the bottom of a page.

- Ensure that the printout is clear and easy to read. Use a new printer cartridge if possible.

- All pages should be secured with a staple in the top left-hand corner. Spiral binding is also acceptable. Do not use a paperclip or pin, as several people may need to handle the assignment before its return to you.

- Carefully proofread any assignments for typographical errors and incorrect grammar. Ask someone else to read your work to see if it is clearly understandable and to check for errors, since your familiarity with the work reduces your ability to read it objectively.

- Check that assignments fulfil the word count requirement. The tolerance on length for most assignments is +/– 10% (10% over or under the word limit). There may be some variations in this allowance between courses, and this should be noted in the assignment instructions; if not stated, adopt the above guideline. Be aware that some instructors may not supply any word limit. Whatever the case, extreme brevity or extreme length will be penalised. **(Note that the word count should not include title page, letter of transmittal, executive summary, tables, figures, appendices or the list of references.)**

- Submit an original copy of the assignment and ensure that a copy is kept for your own records — if an assignment is misplaced, a copy or photocopy of the original will be required.

- Ensure that you make regular backups of the work and that you generate hard-copy printouts regularly. This will allow preliminary versions of the work, or the computer disk containing the work, to be submitted to the instructor, should any last-minute computer problems be encountered. It is unlikely that last-minute extensions will be given because of computer failures without evidence of a partly completed assignment.

- ***Do not*** put assignment pages into folders that have plastic pockets for individual pages. This makes assignments difficult to process. If provided, use assignment cover sheets and labels for your assignment submissions.

1.5 Thesis writing

Thesis writing differs from other forms of academic writing; the thesis writer should consider a number of key issues. The fundamentals of academic writing, such as use of references, use of abbreviations, numbering of tables and figures, and use of capitals and punctuation, remain the same as for other forms of assessable writing. The main difference lies in the area of communication and writing style.

Communication style is of critical importance in thesis writing. While writing your thesis consider what your examiners will be looking for; if you are fortunate enough to know who they will be, find time to read their work and study the way they communicate ideas. In this way you can discover the communication style they prefer and attempt to incorporate this into your own style.

It is important that theses are written as clearly as possible, with changes in direction clearly marked, the line of argument clearly flagged and each step explicitly explained. Most thesis examiners do not read the work in one sitting. They may pick it up and put it down many times in order to fit in the reading among their other commitments. It is therefore essential that thesis writers convey their ideas with the utmost clarity in as structured a form as possible. Do not make the examiners have to think too much, nor send them to sleep; rather, you are hoping that, even if their concentration slips at times, they can check at any time that the thesis is still on track and fulfilling the expectations set up at the start of each section and subsection. In brief, the reader needs to be guided along a smooth, easily followed path towards the conclusions that have excited the writer (Perry 2001).

Students can achieve the kind of easily followed communication essential to thesis writing by adopting five principles. First, introduce new sections and subsections (each with its own descriptive bold heading) as often as every second or third page. Second, start each section or subsection with a phrase or sentence linking it with what has gone before. For example, 'Given the issues discussed in section 1.4 . . .' or 'Turning from international issues to domestic concerns . . .' The important thing to remember is that in this way the examiners are led smoothly from the previous idea to the new one.

Next, briefly introduce and describe at the beginning the argument or point to be made in the section. For example, 'Seven deficiencies in models in the literature will be identified ...' Make each step in the argument easy to follow and identify with a key term in italics or the judicious use of point enumeration ('First', 'Second') or linking words ('Moreover', 'In addition' and so on). Finally, end each section with a summary to establish what it has achieved. This summary sentence or paragraph can be flagged by beginning 'In conclusion ...' or 'In brief ...' These five principles will make your arguments easier to follow and so encourage the examiners towards accepting your views.

The thesis is essentially a long piece of work that develops an idea or concept in depth. It is important that each part of it is carefully considered in terms of its role in the exposition. Each 'chunk', or idea, within the thesis needs to be carefully linked to the other chunks to give continuity to the whole document. Within this concept of chunks and links, think about the role of the paragraph and the sentence. Each paragraph deals with one idea that is introduced in a theme sentence near the start. The start of a paragraph is a 'hot spot' that every reader will focus on (Lindsay 1995). By contrast, each sentence contains one small idea, with the most important part of the sentence presented at the start. Don't waste the 'hot spot' at the start of a sentence or paragraph on unimportant information such as, 'As shown in table 6.1 ...' or 'Smagers and Brown (1998) state ...' Place this sort of reference information at the end of the sentence and use the prime space to communicate a clear idea to the reader. In brief, the thesis should comprise a string of clear chunks of ideas that are well linked in a story line that is easy to follow and understand.

For further information on thesis writing in particular, refer to: Perry, C 1998, 'A structured approach to presenting theses', *Australasian Marketing Journal*, vol. 6, no. 1, pp. 63–85.

1.6 Making the most of the library

1.6.1 What is in the library?

University libraries hold vast numbers of books and thousands of journal titles as well as maps, videos, CD-ROM databases, music cassettes and CDs. Access to databases holding all material is through the library's electronic catalogue. The library is your most important resource as a student.

1.6.2 Finding your way in the library

Most libraries conduct tours to familiarise students with their layout and operation. You are encouraged to attend one of these. Most libraries also conduct classes on how to go about finding information for assignments. Check your individual libraries for times and dates.

Libraries usually hold collections of videos and Computer Aided Learning (CAL) packages that will assist you in learning how to use the library and to research assignments. Look for handouts produced by the library staff on how to research subjects, use databases, reference citations and other useful topics.

1.6.3 Ways to access information

The ways we access information are rapidly changing. Print materials are now complemented by CD-ROM databases. These can help you find references to journal articles and, in the case of full text databases, the articles themselves. There are multimedia CDs offering graphics, text, sound and animation. Libraries also subscribe to electronic databases that can be accessed via their electronic gateways; many sites on the Internet provide a wealth of information. However, newest is not always best, so do not always rely on just one source of information (e.g. using only CD-ROM databases when there might be superior paper indexes).

1.7 Summary

When preparing written work for assessment or review, it is important that students:

- understand and address each of the questions posed in the assessment specifications

- start work on the assignment as soon as possible (avoid the temptation to procrastinate)

- use the resources provided in the library to the greatest extent possible to research the topic or topics

- ensure that their work is presented in accordance with general good practice requirements and the specific requirements of the marker

- ensure that numbers, tables, figures and graphs are presented in a consistent manner and according to the guidelines outlined in this handbook

- proofread their work at least once (preferably more than once) before submission to remove errors such as incorrect punctuation, poor grammar and incorrect spelling

- ensure that slang words and phrases, conversational English and offensive language are not used.

This chapter has presented hints and guidelines relating to each of the preceding points. Having followed the guidelines presented above, students must also cite sources of information included in their work. The next chapter discusses one method by which this can be achieved.

Referencing

2 Referencing

2.1 Introduction

A vital skill that all university students should develop is the ability to critically evaluate existing knowledge and, in so doing, further develop their own understanding of an area of study. Students are often required to demonstrate this ability by producing a written document, such as an essay or report, that interweaves their own ideas and arguments with ideas and arguments documented by other authors.

In order for your work to have depth and credibility, you must demonstrate having read widely on the topic by including information from a range of sources. However, it is important for the reader of the work to know which information in the document has been developed by you, the author, and which information you have borrowed from others. Referencing allows the reader to locate your original source material.

The purpose of referencing in written work is to:

- allow readers of the document to find the original source and learn more about some aspect that the author may have mentioned only briefly in the document

- properly record information sources so that the author can find the original sources of the information used to develop the document should he or she choose to do so at a later time

- provide theoretical support or evidence for statements or conclusions made by the writer

- acknowledge the intellectual property of others and thus avoid the possibility of the author being accused of plagiarism.

Unethical behaviour is discussed in the following section. The chapter then introduces referencing and goes on to provide many practical examples of the Harvard referencing style.

2.2 Unethical behaviour

2.2.1 Plagiarism

The practice of using another writer's ideas or observations and presenting them as your own is called *plagiarism*. Academic writers are expected to be especially vigilant in this regard. Examples of plagiarism include:

- when blocks of text (e.g. paragraphs, sentences, a single sentence or a significant part of a single sentence) are copied directly, but are not enclosed in quotation marks and appropriately referenced

- when direct quotations are not used, but material is paraphrased or summarised in such a way that it substantially reflects ideas taken from another author's work, and the source of the material is not appropriately referenced; and/or

- when an idea that appears in printed or electronic form has been used or developed without reference being made to the person responsible for that idea.[1]

Not plagiarism

'Human resource planning is important because an organisation's effectiveness depends on having the right people in the right jobs at the right times' (Stone 1998, p. 49). If an organisation doesn't ...

Plagiarism

Human resource planning is important because an organisation's effectiveness depends on having the right people in the right jobs at the right times. If an organisation doesn't ...

If you directly quote an author's words, you must acknowledge that these are not your words by using quotation marks and giving the author's name, date of publication and page number. If you do not acknowledge the original source of the words, you are committing plagiarism.

Not plagiarism

Human resource planning is important because organisations need to have appropriate people in appropriate jobs at a time when they are needed (Stone 1998). If organisations don't ...

Plagiarism

Human resource planning is important because organisations need to have appropriate people in appropriate jobs at a time when they are needed. If organisations don't ...

If what you say is almost the same as what the author said but you have changed a few words, you must acknowledge that these are basically someone else's words by giving the author's name and the date of publication. This is called *paraphrasing*. If you do not do acknowledge the original source of the words, you are guilty of plagiarism.

Not plagiarism

If organisations are to function as well as possible, they need to make sure that staff are available to fill jobs when the need arises (Stone 1998). If they don't ensure this ...

---

1. We gratefully acknowledge contribution to the development of this section on plagiarism by Dr Lesley Willcoxon.

As Stone (1998) states, if organisations are to function as well as possible, they need to make sure that staff are available to fill jobs when the need arises. If they don't ensure this ...

Plagiarism

If organisations are to function as well as possible, they need to make sure that staff are available to fill jobs when the need arises. If they don't ensure this ...

If you use someone else's ideas, you must acknowledge that these are not your own original ideas by giving the author's name and the date of publication of the source material. In the case above, Stone makes the same point in several places throughout the book so it is not necessary to provide a specific page number. If you do not acknowledge the original source of the ideas, you are guilty of plagiarism.

Plagiarism is cheating and is totally unacceptable in university work. In written work submitted for assessment in most universities, plagiarism may lead not only to assignment failure but also to proceedings under the university's academic regulations (see your Student Handbook).

2.2.2 Collusion

The practice of working in groups to share ideas, either formally or informally, is accepted and encouraged as an approach to learning in university study. However, all assignments must be submitted individually unless students are specifically directed otherwise. It is **not** acceptable, unless otherwise clearly stipulated in writing by the course examiner, for two or more students to submit identical work, or to submit copies of work done as a group. Examiners are entitled to consider identical layout, identical mistakes, identical argument and identical presentation as prima facie evidence of collusion.

In general, students should ensure that they have a very clear understanding of the submission requirements of each course by carefully reading the instructions.

2.3 Referencing — general information

2.3.1 When to provide a reference

A reference is required in the following instances:

- **Direct quotation**
  When another writer's work is quoted verbatim (word for word). Whether a phrase, sentence or paragraph, the quote must be enclosed in single quotation marks and a reference to the source provided.

- **Paraphrasing/summarising**
  Ideas or data obtained from another writer must be referenced — *even if the wording and/or context has been changed*.

- **Controversial information, opinions or data that an informed reader might challenge**
  If, for example, an author states that Australia was first discovered by Europeans in 1522 (instead of much later, as is commonly accepted), the author will have to support that assertion by acknowledging the source of the information.

- **Tables, figures, diagrams and appendices**
  When statistical data, diagrams or illustrations are either taken whole or adapted from another source, that source must be cited.

In short, students must reference any ideas or data that are not their own. Information of a general nature, such as facts and ideas that are common knowledge, do not need references. For example, that the Commonwealth of Australia was created in 1901 is well known and undisputed, so no reference is required in this case.

2.3.2 Referencing — a helpful hint

It is always much easier to record the complete and correct reference for sources used in works at the time the information is first found. Therefore, when making photocopies of information to be used in assignments, always ensure that *at the time of photocopying* you collect *all the source information* you will require to cite the source properly. The best way to do this is either to photocopy the title and copyright pages of the book or journal containing the article, or to simply hand-write the relevant information on the photocopy. Furthermore, when transcribing or using information from a source, you should get into the habit of inserting the complete reference *at the time the information is transcribed or viewed*. Trying to find the necessary information later can be a frustrating task.

Remember, also, that when you are using references and quotations to support your discussion in written work, you must summarise in your own words the significance of the quotation and how it adds to, or supports, your argument/view. You need to show the reader that you have understood the meaning of the referenced work; you should not leave it for the reader to try to work out how the reference or quotation relates to your discussion.

2.4 Methods of referencing

The primary purpose of referencing is to enable the reader to easily locate the source of material taken from other authors' work. Therefore it is important, first, that the author provides the reader with *all relevant information for each source* and, second, that the information is presented in a *consistent format* throughout the document.

Information published using traditional paper-based methods is static once printed and is therefore relatively easy to cite. Many methods of referencing have been developed to facilitate a standard approach to the task. Commonly used methods include the Harvard system (also known as the author–date system), the Chicago system (also known as the footnoting system) and the Vancouver system, although many other systems are in use. This guide will focus on examples using the Harvard system.

Some methods are preferred, and in some cases mandated, by various disciplines but are not favoured by others. Occasionally, even journals within the same discipline may use conflicting referencing methods.

The recent rise in electronic publishing has made the task of appropriately referencing sources of information more complex. Information that must be recorded about electronically published material differs from that required for paper-based material. This is mainly because of the different ways that electronic information is represented and accessed compared with traditional methods. Information published in electronic form has the potential to be highly dynamic. First, in the case of Internet sources, information may change from day to day, or even minute to minute. Information available to someone accessing a particular site at 9.00 am may differ greatly from information available from the same site at 10.00 pm on the same day. Second, the location of information is also subject to change.

Because computers require precision, the author must take particular care to ensure that the names of Internet sites are recorded accurately, in terms of both spelling and capitalisation. Standards for citing electronic material are still developing, but a section describing the current required approach to referencing electronic material has been included in this handbook.

Rules and examples pertaining to presentation of in-text references and lists of references are included in the following sections.

The explanations and examples provided cover the commonly occurring situations only, and are therefore not exhaustive. For a more detailed introduction to referencing, students should refer to chapter 12 of the *Style manual* (2002).

2.5 The Harvard system

Authors using the Harvard system must include **both** of the following for each citation:

- an in-text reference (acknowledgement in the main body of the document)
- a corresponding entry in the list of references (a list of all the sources cited in the report, with the exception of personal communications).

2.6 In-text references

This section describes how to insert references in the body of the text using the Harvard referencing system.

2.6.1 Format

An in-text reference includes:

- the surname(s) of the author(s) of the work
- the year the work was published
- (where appropriate) the page number(s) where the cited information can be found in the publication.

Note: A page number is required if you are referring to a direct quotation or to figures/data produced in a research project.

In general, it is advisable not to begin a sentence or paragraph with a citation to authorities.

 In a recent research report by Smith, Brown, Adams and Zikopoelus (1999) it was suggested that marketing is the key functional area of any business.

Better,

 Marketing is the key functional area of any business (Smith, Brown, Adams & Zikopoelus 1999).

The year and page number(s), when provided, are always enclosed within parentheses. The name of the author(s) may or may not be enclosed in parentheses depending on the circumstance (see examples above). Specific in-text referencing rules and examples (citing paper-based sources) follow.

2.6.2 When to include page numbers

The page number must be included in the reference when directly quoting a block of text or when including statistical data from a source. Page numbers are not usually necessary (check your assignment instructions) when paraphrasing or borrowing a general theme or idea from a work.

When including page numbers, the correct format for one page is 'p. 6'. For two or more pages 'pp. 23–37' should be used (*Style manual* 2002, p. 194). Page numbers should indicate where the quote starts and finishes. If the start and finish page numbers are in the same decimal range (e.g. 20 and 29, or 322 and 328), the finishing page number should include only the relevant final digits of the number (e.g. 20–9 or 322–8).

In cases in which quotes run over non-consecutive pages, 'pp.' should be used and the page numbers should be separated by a comma. The following examples illustrate the use of page numbers.

 (Wells 1999, p. 4) — note the position of the comma after the year

(Smith 1998, pp. 1, 4, 6) — i.e. pages 1, 4 and 6

(Jones & Mackey 2000, pp. 25–6) — i.e. pages 25 to 26

(Arbut, King & Browning 1999, pp. 459–87) — i.e. pages 459 to 487

2.6.3 Footnotes

Although footnotes are permissible in the Harvard system, they are *not* used for citing sources. Footnotes may be used for providing information that is incidental to the main argument in the text. For example, a footnote could be used to expand on or explain a term or a point raised that is relevant but, if included in the main body of the text, would interrupt the flow of the discourse. Terms such as *op. cit., ibid.* and *id.* are **not** used in the Harvard system.

2.6.4 Short quotations

Direct quotes should be enclosed in ***single*** quotation marks. If the quote does not begin at the start of a sentence, the author should use three dots (an ellipsis) to convey this to the reader. Ellipses should also be used to indicate when the remainder of a sentence quoted is not included. See Section 1.3.7 for more information on ellipses and the following pages for examples.

2.6.5 Long quotations

Where direct quotes exceed 30 words they should be indented from the left margin and single line spaced ***without*** quotation marks. The quote should be introduced by a colon, and one line space should separate the quote from the introductory statement and from the text that follows. The quote should be set one point size smaller than the font used for the main text (*Style manual* 2002, p. 113). See Section 2.6.6 for an example.

2.6.6 Single author

The following examples show how to include in-text references for sources with one author.

The population of Amitamia in 2000 was 17.6 million (Hogg 2002, p. 35).

Johnson (2001, p. 27) stated that '... lack of exercise is our most serious problem'.

The incidence of coronary disease in Australian males has increased in the past ten years (Williams 2001).

Tanenbaum (2000, p. 1) has the following to say about technological evolution:

> Each of the past three centuries has been dominated by a single technology. The 18th Century was the time of great mechanical systems accompanying the Industrial Revolution. The 19th Century was the age of the steam engine. During the 20th Century, the key technology has been information gathering, processing and distribution.

2.6.7 Two or more authors

When a work has two authors, **both** names should be included in every citation (*Style manual* 2002, ch. 12); the authors' names should be separated by an ampersand (&) if enclosed in parentheses, or separated by 'and' if the names are outside the parentheses (see the examples below). Where three or more authors are cited, the same format applies except that the first two (or more) names are separated by a comma and only the last two names are separated by '&'.

Where there are more than three authors, to enhance the readability of the text only the first author's name need be included followed by 'et al.' (meaning 'and others'). In cases where there are different combinations of authors with the same first author, **all** names should be used in **all** citations to avoid confusion. Initials should be used in the citation only in situations where two different authors share the same surname.

It has been recently revealed that zebras are not native to Africa (Hichell & Williams 2000). ... Hichell and Williams (2001) now contend that zebras originated in Iceland. Other authors dispute this statement (Williams, HM 2002).

Here two authors share the surname Williams and the use of initials allows the reader to differentiate between them.

Network technologies have become increasingly complex in recent times (Cook, Burger & Brown 2000). ... Local area networks are now very common (Samson et al. 2001).

Here '(Samson et al. 2001)' refers to a 2001 publication by Samson, Thames, Burger, Brown and Cook.

2.6.8 Two or more works in one citation

When two or more works are included in one citation, they should be arranged in alphabetical order and delimited by a semicolon.

The decrease in the zebra population appears to be related to an increase in technological innovation (Cook, Burger & Brown 2001; Hichell & Williams 2001).

When two or more works from the same author are cited, they should be listed in chronological order.

The zebra population in Africa is declining (Hichell & Williams 1998, 1999, 2000).

When two or more works from the same author in the same year are cited, append a, b, c etc. to the year. This should reflect the order presented in the list of references.

Local area networks are used by more and more organisations (Bruin 2001a, 2001b).

2.6.9 Newspapers

Newspapers should be cited as shown in the following examples (note italics and omission of 'The' from the newspaper title).

The following example shows how a newspaper article whose author is not known should include all details in the in-text citation. In this case, no entry is required in the list of references (*Style manual* 2002, p. 206), as follows:

 A new American president has been elected (*Weekend Australian* 24–25 February 2001). ... In the *Financial Review* (25 July 2002, p. 23).

If the author of the article is known, then the author–year format should be used, and the reference provided in the list of references.

 A new American president has been elected (Bloggs 2001).

For frequent references to the same newspaper material, abbreviations are acceptable. For example, the *Sydney Morning Herald* is shortened to *SMH*.

2.6.10 Personal communications

A corresponding entry in the list of references is not required for personal communications, since they cannot be retrieved by the reader. However, the author's surname, initials, 'pers. comm.' and the date of the communication must be included in the text. You must also be sure to obtain permission from the person being referred to. Note that the initials of the person *precede* the family name.

 A survey is currently being undertaken by John Smith to ascertain the acceptance of electronic payment methods in the community (J Smith 2001, pers. comm., 15 May).

When interviewed on 22 September, Mr P Frank admitted that the major problems for Telstra's marketing division were coming from the organisation's recent expansion. Mr P Frank (Telstra marketing manager) confirmed the press rumours by facsimile on 15 May 2002.

This is also the format used for e-mail communications, although you should be careful to verify the source of the e-mail communication before citing it as a personal communication.

Note: Students should not quote statements made by lecturers or tutors unless the information quoted has been officially published. External study guides and notes are considered by most universities to be official publications, and any material taken from them must be acknowledged.

2.6.11 Anonymous works

In cases where the author's name is not available, 'anonymous' should **not** be used. Either the sponsoring organisation (see Section 2.6.13) or the title of the article (in italics) should be included. When determining the alphabetical order of these references, ignore words at the start of the title such as 'a', 'an' or 'the'.

 Large numbers of organisations are now using the Internet as a marketing tool *(The web as a marketing tool* 2002).

2.6.12 Publication date unavailable

If the publication date of a source cannot be ascertained, 'n.d.' may be used or, where it is possible to approximate the date of publication, '*c.*' (from the Latin *circa,* meaning 'about'*)* may be used.

 It seems that technology has encouraged people to lead sedentary lives (Moorbent n.d.). Althaus (*c.* 1999, p. 2) supported this assertion and stated that ' … in today's society … because of computers'.

2.6.13 Sponsoring organisation

When there is no specific author, but the name of the organisation sponsoring the publication is available, the organisation's name should be included.

 In a publication by the University of Southern Queensland (1996), the Vice Chancellor said …

In a recent report it was stated that '… raging dry season bushfires are easily the most dramatic feature of the Australian scene' (Department of Primary Industries 2000, p. 56).

2.6.14 Unpublished works

When students cite an unpublished source, such as a letter, minutes of a meeting or a company report, the in-text reference guidelines are the same as for journals and periodicals. That is, the author or sponsoring organisation, and the year of publication (if known) are included. Other in-text referencing rules apply if no publication date is available (see Section 2.6.12), if the work is anonymous (see Section 2.6.11) or if more than one work by the same author is cited (see Section 2.6.8).

 The changes to the structure of the organisation were not only planned, but also strategically motivated as evidenced in the intercompany fax between the managing director and the union representative (Harrison 2001).

It was evident from the minutes of the July meeting (National Teachers Union 2002) that many teachers were unaware of the implications of the decision to accept the changes proposed by the federal government.

2.6.15 Citations for sources other than the original

Books of readings

In the case of material taken from a book of readings, students are required to inform the reader that the material cited is not taken from the original source. This should be done through an appropriate entry in the list of references (see Section 2.7.4 for further explanation). The in-text citation references the original source of the material as shown below.

 Stallings and Van Slyke (in Cappel 2000) defined a digital signal as '... a sequence of voltage pulses that may be transmitted over a wire medium ...'

Indirect quotations

In general, students must make every attempt to discover the original source of a quotation. However, there may be instances when the original source is inaccessible for some reason (e.g. it is out of print) or the original source is in a foreign language. In these cases it is permissible to use an indirect quote from another source. The original author, year of publication and page number(s) (where appropriate) should be quoted in the in-text reference in the normal manner. However, both the original source and the indirect source should be included in the list of references entry and should be separated by the words 'cited in' to acknowledge that an indirect quotation has been used (see Section 2.7 for an example of the list of references (LOR) entry).

2.6.16 Tables and figures either extracted or taken whole

When tables or figures are extracted or presented in their entirety in documents, the reference should:

- be presented using the same format as that used in a list of references for that type of source
- be preceded by 'Source:'
- be enclosed in parentheses
- include the page number(s) preceded by 'p.' or 'pp.' as appropriate.

The following example shows a table taken in its entirety from a *book*:

Animal	Population (1990)	Population (1995)	Population (2000)
Zebra	300 000	270 000	250 000
Lion	60 000	65 000	68 000

(*Source:* Edwards et al. 2000, p. 67)

If some parts of the table were taken from another author's work, but other parts were added (e.g. a column or row added to the table, or only part of the table included), then the word 'Source:' should be replaced by 'Adapted from:' and the reference or references for multiple sources provided.

2.7 List of references (LOR) entries for paper-based sources — specific rules and examples

Authors using the Harvard system must include in-text references **and** either a list of references or a bibliography. In both a list of references and a bibliography, publications are listed in **alphabetical order** based on authors' surnames. Multiple references to the same author should be listed in chronological order.

A list of references differs from a bibliography in the following way: Only sources actually **cited** in the main body of the text are included in a list of references. All references used in the preparation of the document, whether or not they are cited, are listed in a bibliography.

Unless specifically directed by their course examiner to do otherwise, students are advised to include a list of references with written work — that is, only sources actually cited in the work should be included.

Titles of books and articles should be listed using minimal capitalisation. The original title, as used on the cover, should be preserved in the reference.

Full stops and spaces are not used with initials, and book and periodical names are italicised.

The second and subsequent lines of each entry should be indented to enhance readability.

Examples of how to include commonly occurring items in a list of references (LOR) are provided in the following pages.

2.7.1 LOR — book citation

The general format for including a book entry in a list of references is as follows:

> <Author's surname>, <Author's initial(s) — no spaces between initials if more than one> <year of publication>, in <editor, reviser, compiler or translator if applicable>, <*Title of publication*>, <edition abbreviated as edn, e.g. 2nd edn>, <volume number if applicable, abbreviated as vol.>, <publisher>, <place of publication>, <page number if applicable>.

The title of the publication is italicised. Where there are two authors, the names are separated by '&'. For more than two authors, all surnames are separated by a comma, other than the final two, which are separated by an ampersand (&). The abbreviation 'ed.' is used to indicate one editor, and 'eds' is used to indicate more than one editor. *Edition* is abbreviated to 'edn'.

Brady, J 2001, *International marketing*, Prentice Hall, Toronto.

Michael, F & Emming, BM 1991, *Strategic planning*, 3rd edn, Prentice Hall, London.

Cranbourne, CA, Keane, B & Sumner, CC 2000, *African wildlife*, Irwin, Chicago.

Campbell, HB (ed.) 2001, *Internet Information sources*, Pergamon Press, Oxford.

2.7.2 LOR — article or chapter in an edited book

The same format is used here as above, except that the author of the chapter or article is acknowledged first, the title of the article or chapter is enclosed in single quotation marks, and the editors are included before the title of the book. It should also be noted that the editors' initials precede their surname. The word 'in' is also included to indicate that the chapter is contained within a book and is not the title of the book.

 Axelsson, B & Easton, G 1992, 'Foreign market entry — The textbook vs. the network theory', in B Axelsson & G Easton (eds), *Industrial networks: a new view of reality,* Routledge, London, pp. 46–59.

2.7.3 LOR — study notes

Study notes should be listed in the same manner as a book.

 Smith, B 2000, *Networks and distributed systems study book*, Distance Education Centre, USQ, Toowoomba, Australia.

The following format applies where the author's name is not known:

 Networks and distributed systems study book 2000, Distance Education Centre, USQ, Toowoomba, Australia.

2.7.4 LOR — books of readings

In the case of books of readings, students are required to include ***both*** a reference to the original article and a reference to the book of readings from which the article was sourced, as shown in the example below. This will allow the reader to obtain the material from either source.

 Stallings, W & Van Slyke, R 2000, 'Signal encoding', *Business data communications*, 2nd edn, Prentice Hall, New Jersey, p. 28, cited in B Smith (ed.), *Networks and Distributed Systems Selected Readings* 2001, Distance Education Centre, USQ, Toowoomba, Australia. Reading 3.1.

2.7.5 LOR — indirect quotation

When a source is quoted in the text but that source is not the original source of the quotation, the following format should be used.

 Galvin, P 2002, *Electronic principles*, cited in Stallings, W & Van Slyke, R 2002, 'Signal encoding', *Business data communications*, 2nd edn, Macmillan College Publishing Company Inc., New York, p. 23.

2.7.6 LOR — article in journal

Articles require the same basic format as books, except that the title of the article is enclosed in single quotes, a volume number (abbreviated to 'vol.') and series number (abbreviated to 'no.') for the journal is included, and page numbers are added. Sometimes a series number is not available, but a season such as 'Autumn' or 'Summer', or a period such as 'March/May' may be used instead.

> Major, A, Ng, DG & Barr, NW 2001, 'A proposition-based approach to a market exit strategy', *Journal of International Marketing*, vol. 3, no. 5, pp. 69–87.
>
> Dennis, R 2000, 'Theory and practice in marketing research', *Journal of Marketing*, vol. 27, Summer, pp. 131–40.
>
> Andresson, H & Crewes, LP 1999, 'International market channels of distribution', *Journal of Marketing*, vol. 34, January, pp. 71–82.

2.7.7 LOR — sponsoring organisation

Sometimes a specific author is not known. In this case the sponsoring organisation may be used.

> Bureau of Transport Economics 2001, *Economic regulations of aviation in Australia*, seminar papers and proceedings, AGPS, Canberra.
>
> Austrade 2000, 'Exporting of services comes into focus', *Business Review Weekly*, September 17, p. 1.

2.7.8 LOR — multiple publications by the same author

Where several works by the same author are listed, the author's name may be replaced by a 2-em rule (see *Style manual* 2002, pp. 194–5) in the second and subsequent entries in the list of references. For works by the same author in the same year, an alphabetic suffix is appended to the year (e.g. '1999a', '1999b').

> Sheridan, G 1985, 'Children and education', *Courier-Mail*, 3 Mar., p. 2.
> —— 1985a, 'Early childhood learning', *Weekend Australian*, 4 Aug., p. 5.
> —— 1985b, 'Our youngsters', *Weekend Australian*, 4 Dec., p. 7.
> —— & Smith, L 1986, 'The education system exposed', *Business Review Weekly*, 4 Jan., p. 5.

2.7.9 LOR — conference paper, working paper series and thesis

For papers presented to conferences but not published in proceedings, the correct format is as follows:

> Ritchie, JB 2002, 'Accessing international education markets', paper presented to 3rd Internationalising Education Conference, Sydney, 22–23 Sept.

For papers presented at a conference and published in conference proceedings the format is as follows:

 DuPont, B 2001, 'Marketing and the Internet: Implications for managers', *Proceedings of the third annual Australian Marketing Association*, Melbourne, Australian Marketing Association, Melbourne, Australia, pp. 44–6.

Working paper series:

 Selvarajah, CT 1988, 'Marketing education in Malaysia: implications for Australian tertiary institutions', *Faculty of Business & Commerce staff papers*, Working Paper no. 43, Swinburne Institute of Technology, Melbourne.

Theses:

 Crowley, FK 1999, 'Working class conditions in Australia, 1788–1851', PhD thesis, University of Melbourne.

Naudi, A 2000, 'Change management', MIT thesis, University of Southern Queensland.

2.7.10 LOR — article in newspaper or magazine
The format for newspaper or magazine articles is very similar to that used for journals.

 Austrade 1993, 'Exporting of services comes into focus', *Business Review Weekly*, September 17, p. 1.

Keating, P 1999, 'The "quiet revolution"', *Asian Business Review*, April, pp. 16–17.

The New Straits Times 2001, 'One more time', 24 January, p. 32.

2.7.11 LOR — unpublished works
For unpublished works, such as papers presented at seminars, manuscripts, letters, faxes and reports, the following guidelines apply for the list of references. (Unpublished electronic works such as e-mails are addressed in Section 2.9.7.) The author's name and the year of preparation of the document are presented in the manner described for articles in journals and periodicals. The title of the work (if appropriate) should also be presented in the same manner, but without quotation marks. Other details should be provided with a view to guiding the reader as efficiently as possible. These details will vary according to the nature of the document. Personal communications need not be included in lists of references, but are cited in the text itself.

Harrison, Q 2001, planning requirements for restructure, Brisbane Chamber of Commerce and Industry, fax to J Golding, 24 July.

Cranbourne, F 2002, Western Computer Supplies, letter to George Wilson, Queensland Secretary, Australian Manufacturing Workers Union, 24 April.

Insurance Council of Australia 2001, submission to the Committee of Inquiry into Workers' Compensation in Victoria, workers' compensation report, Melbourne, 19 December.

National Teachers Union, Brisbane Branch 2002, minutes of branch committee meeting, Brisbane, 2 June.

2.8 Electronic referencing method

Traditional paper-based referencing methods are not adequate for appropriately citing works that have been published using electronic methods. A number of scholars have proposed methods for referencing electronic documents (Li & Crane 1993; 1996; *Electronic sources: APA style of citation* n.d.; *Electronic sources: MLA style of citation* n.d.; Lamp n.d.; Page 1996) and the *Style manual* (2002) also deals with the issue on pages 230–1.

It is important for students to maintain as much consistency as possible between the referencing system used for paper-based works and that used for electronic works. There are a number of methods that follow either APA (American Psychological Association) or MLA (Modern Language Association) style. Here, we will focus on those based on the Harvard format.

2.8.1 Electronic referencing — general information

As previously described for paper-based referencing (see Section 2.4), two components are required when referencing electronic sources of information; namely, an in-text reference and a corresponding entry in the list of references at the end of the document.

2.8.2 In-text references — electronic sources

When referencing electronic information, the Harvard format should be used for in-text references. The name of the author, or the title of the article, or the name of the sponsoring organisation (if the author is unknown), should be included along with the year and the relevant page numbers, if applicable. If citing a URL, the date of the last update should be given. The use of angle brackets (< >) around the URL is recommended.

When the author is known and the page numbers are relevant:

People are now living longer than they did a century ago (Brown 2001). This finding has been further supported by Smith (2002, p. 4), who stated that ...

When the author is unknown and the sponsoring organisation is relevant:

 As a direct result of pollution, vegetation is dying on the hillsides (Australian Conservation Foundation 2002).

When the author is unknown and a URL is provided (note: rather than a year, the last date the site was updated is given):

 Sporting events now constitute 9 out of 10 most watched television programs in American history (<http://www.baysider.com/Features/superbowl.html>, March 2001).

2.8.3 LOR — electronic sources, general

Generally speaking, entries in the list of references should follow the Harvard system (see Sections 2.6 and 2.7). However, owing to the dynamic nature of electronic publishing, additional information must be included when citing references for works published using this medium.

If the information was obtained from the Internet, the address of the site where the information was stored (in angled brackets < >) and the date when the information was accessed (prefixed by 'viewed') should be included. This warns the reader that the information, or facts and figures included in the text by the author, was current on the stated site on the date it was accessed by the author, but that changes in the content or location of the information may have occurred since that date.

Some examples are included below to illustrate how different types of electronic material should be cited.

2.9 LOR entries for electronic sources — specific rules and examples

2.9.1 CD-ROM — book

Note that Microsoft is the producer of the CD-ROM in the first example that follows, and that the date is the date of production of the CD-ROM. The date of access is not required for a CD-ROM because, like paper-based material, the information on any particular edition will not change after it has been published.

 Clark, MK 2000, *Birds of Australia*, CD-ROM, 2nd edn, Microsoft Corporation.

'The American Presidents' 2001, in *The 2000 Grolier Multimedia Encyclopedia*, CD-ROM, ver. 7, Grolier Incorporated, 1995.

2.9.2 Database — journal

Wallace, B 2000, 'Microwave, infrared products target LANs', *Computerworld*, CD-ROM, vol. 31, no. 4, p. 56, viewed 20 March 2003, ABI/INFORM database, item: 1364220.

Anderson, H 2000, 'Turning intranets into strategic marketing weapons', *Network World*, vol. 14, no. 4, p. 4, viewed 20 March 2003, EBSCOhost database, Business Source Elite, item: 01363555.

Note that 'item' in the above examples refers to the accession number of the article on the database. This number is an index and provides fast access to the document when using the database. Also note that you need to provide the date the database was viewed.

2.9.3 Internet sites (author and date available)

Lee, MT 2000, *Guidelines for citing references and electronic sources of information*, viewed 12 May 2001, <http://www.eliz.tased.edu.au/refs.htm>.

Note that the address of the web site must be included and preceded by 'viewed'. Care must be taken to ensure that the capitalisation and spelling of the address of the site is preserved exactly.

2.9.4 Internet sites (author and date not available)

Guidelines for citing references and electronic sources of information (n.d.), viewed 12 May 2000 <http://www.eliz.tased.edu.au/refs.htm>.

2.9.5 FTP sites

Smith, MT 2000, *Electronic sources of information*, viewed 5 April 2001, <ftp://ftp.usq.edu.au/refs.doc>.

2.9.6 Discussion group message

The general format for citing a discussion list message is as follows:

<Author> <Author's identifying details — usually e-mail address> <Date when message was posted>, <Title of posting>, *<Discussion Group Name>*, <Discussion group owner>, <Date of viewing>, <URL>.

Brown, F <brownf@bigbrain.com> 2000, 'Using the Web more efficiently', discussion group, National Computer Network, viewed 23 April 2001, <observe@abc.net.com>.

2.9.7 Personal e-mail message

Normally, e-mail messages are not included in the list of references and they are treated the same way as personal communications (see Section 2.6.10). Where it is necessary, however, the general format for citing a personal e-mail message is as follows:

> <Sender's name with initial preceding surname>, <e-mail>, <Date of e-mail>, <e-mail address>.

A Elsworth, e-mail, 10 August 1999, <elswortha@ugt.edu.au>.

Note: it is critical that you obtain the sender's permission before publishing their e-mail address.

2.10 Films, videos and television

The title, date of recording, format, publisher, place of recording and any special credits should be listed (*Style manual* 2002, p. 229) as shown in the following examples.

Film:

Learning to live 2000, motion picture, London, Fine Films Inc., Producer Martin Freeth.

Video recording or television:

What are we going to do with the money?, video recording, ABC Television, Sydney, 8 August 2000.

2.11 Summary

To prepare a well-balanced written assignment, wide reading and research is required. Interpretation of the thoughts, ideas and research findings of other writers is essential. This process allows the development of a personal perspective on the topic and gives the written work credibility and depth. Referencing serves the professional purpose of allowing subsequent researchers to re-analyse and re-interpret the written work if they choose to work on the topic or issue.

However, material included from other sources must be correctly referenced or the author may be accused of plagiarism. Correct referencing is not only an ethical requirement of any written work, it is a legal one.

The important points to note from this chapter are:

1 Plagiarism and collusion are unacceptable.

2 Students must:

- reference other authors' material used in written assignment work by providing both in-text references and a list of references

- use the methods described in this handbook when formatting in-text references and lists of references.

2.12 Example of the Harvard referencing system

Below is an example of how to use the Harvard system.

> You'd hear them passing in the street, front doors closing, soft voices, muffled footsteps. Then the first mill whistles at seven o'clock, telling you it was time to get up. Those whistles regulated your life, whether or not you worked in the mills. I never got used to it when they stopped. (Glenda Jansen 1998, pers. comm., 23 June)

The textile mills of Geelong were mostly silent during the early 1970s, when the full effects of the downturn in the textile industry were felt. Geelong's textile workforce was virtually halved, and sackings ran at 60 per day over 1975 (Anderson 1977; *Geelong Advertiser* 1974). The Textile Workers Union had 3 364 members in the Geelong district in 1971; two years later this number had dropped to 1 398 (Hughes 1977, p. 10).

The decline led inevitably to widespread mill closures. Another notable consequence was a shift in the division of labour: men, who constituted only 42 percent of the workforce in the mills operating in 1961 (Australian Textile Workers Union 1961), comprised a 61 percent majority in 1986 (Australian Bureau of Statistics 1986).

The painful restructuring during these years had a traumatic impact on both male- and female-dominated areas of employment. While women in the textile, clothing and footwear industries were laid off in increasing numbers, men in the car and aluminium industries were equally hard hit during the global rationalisation that followed the oil crises of the 1970s (Hughes 1977; Linge & McKay 1981; Rich 1987).

List of References

Anderson, H 1977, 'The mill workers of the 1970s', *Network World*, vol. 14, no. 4, p. 4, viewed 10 March 2002, ABI/INFORM database, item: 01363555.

Australian Bureau of Statistics 1986, *Census of population and housing. Local government area, Geelong statistical district*, Australian Government Publishing Service, Canberra.

Australian Textile Workers Union 1961, weekly employment records in Geelong by mill, unpublished report.

Geelong Advertiser 1974, 'All in a day's work', Monday 24 July, p. 30.

Hughes, W 1977, 'The state of the textile industry', *Textile Topics*, vol. 1, no. 16, pp. 10–12.

Linge, G & McKay, J 1981, *Structural change in Australia: some spatial and organisational responses*, HG/15 Research School of Pacific Studies, Canberra.

Rich, D 1987, *The industrial geography of Australia*, Methuen, North Ryde, NSW.

(Adapted from Deakin University 1993, *Faculty of Arts style guide*, Geelong, pp. 10–11)

2.13 Bibliography

The following references were used to prepare this chapter. Readers who want more information on referencing may also find these useful.

Commonwealth of Australia 2002, *Style manual for authors, editors and printers*, 6th edn, John Wiley & Sons, Brisbane.

Electronic sources: APA style of citation (n.d.), viewed 6 May 1997, <http:// www.uvm.edu /~ncrane/estyles/apa.html>.

Electronic sources: MLA style of citation (n.d.), viewed 6 May 1997, <http:// www.uvm.edu /~ncrane/estyles/mla.html>.

Guides to citing electronic information (n.d.), viewed 6 May 1997, <http:// mahogany.lib.utexas.edu/Libs/PCL/Cite.html>.

ISO 1997, *Excerpts from final draft International Standard ISO 690-2*, viewed 9 May 1997, <http://www.nlc-bnc.ca/iso/tc46sc9/standard/690-2e.htm>.

Lamp, J (n.d.), *Citation styles for electronic media*, viewed 9 May 1997, <http// lamp.cs.utas.edu.au/citation.html>.

Lee, MT 1996, *Guidelines for citing references and electronic sources of Information*, viewed 6 May 1997, <http://www.eliz.tased.edu.au/refs.htm>.

Li, X & Crane, NB 1993, *Electronic style: a guide to citing electronic information*, Mecklermedia, Westport, CT.

Page, ME 1996, *A brief citation guide for Internet sources in history and the humanities*, viewed 9 May 1997, ver. 2.1, <http://h-net2.msu.edu/~africa/ citation.html>.

Referencing Internet resources using the Harvard system (n.d.), viewed 8 May 1997, <http://www.usq.edu.au/library/pubsexms/elecinfo/citing1.htm>.

Walker, JR 1996, *MLA-style citations of electronic sources*, viewed 6 May 1997, <http://www.cas.usf.edu/english/walker/mla.html>.

Note: The following (revised) edition of Li and Crane (1993) is now available:

Li, X & Crane, NB 1996, *Electronic style: a guide to citing electronic information*, Information Today, Medford, NJ.

Report writing

3 | Report writing[2]

3.1 Introduction

All written assignments must follow specific structures that allow the document to be easily read and understood. This chapter provides a useful guide for students preparing written work in a formal report format. A formal report should contain the following sections, in the order given:

1. Assignment cover sheet
2. Letter of transmittal (not always required)
3. Title page
4. Executive summary
5. Table of contents
6. Introduction
7. The body
8. Conclusions
9. Recommendations (sometimes not required)
10. List of references
11. Glossary (not always required)
12. Appendices

3.2 Report structure

This section will provide detailed guidance on each section of the formal report as listed above.

3.2.1 Assignment cover sheet

The cover sheet protects the assignment and identifies the student and the due date. It also provides verification of submission date and authentication of original work through the student's signature. This signature on the statement of original work is legally binding and means that the student agrees that any non-original work in the assignment has been appropriately referenced.

3.2.2 Letter of transmittal

A letter of transmittal enables the writer of the report to establish contact with the receiver, and acts as the formal record of delivery of the report.

The letter of transmittal should be fully left-justified (with the exception of the sender's address) and should use open punctuation (no commas or full stops in the address or heading section of the letter). In general, letters of transmittal use single spacing within the parts of the letter and double spacing between the parts (i.e. paragraphs or heading and greeting). See Figure 3.1 for an example.

2. We gratefully acknowledge contribution to this section by Mr Cec Pederson.

Blair Consultants
122 Arthur Street
TOWNSVILLE QLD 4810
14 July 2001

Mr Warren Vale
NewIdeas Pty Ltd
54 Phillip Street
TOWNSVILLE QLD 4810

Dear Mr Vale

Further to your request of 23 July, I hereby attach our report analysing the market potential for the new product you are assessing. As discussed with you during our meeting last month, we have paid particular attention in our analysis to the consumer decision-making processes of your target market.

The report provides a detailed breakdown of the product's possible impact in the marketplace, as well as a full examination of your direct and indirect competitors.

Our investigations suggest that this product has good market potential in the current economic conditions. However, as outlined in our report, indications of possible competition from South-East Asian producers within the next decade suggest the need for an accelerated development program in order to establish a niche in the new market. We recommend that your company proceed with the development of the product, with consideration given to the revised schedule provided in this report.

We have proposed a number of ways in which you might counter potential foreign competition while maximising your domestic sales profile. None of these proposals, we believe, need affect product development, but several suggestions hold the promise of broadening the potential domestic market in surprising directions. We discuss these points in detail in the report.

Thank you for affording us the opportunity to work with you on this project. I will be glad to discuss any questions you may have at our meeting next week.

Yours sincerely

M. Ehrlich

Martin Ehrlich — Director

FIGURE 3.1 Example of a letter of transmittal

The letter should be addressed to the person who requested the report (in your assignments it is permissible to use a fictitious person), and the return address of the sender should be left-justified, unless official letterhead is used (your name should not appear at this point). The city/state elements of the sender's return address and of the receiver's address should be entered in capital letters.

The date of writing should be in the format *day/month/year*, with the month written in full and not abbreviated as a number (e.g. *3 March 1994*, and not *3/3/94*). Avoid the use of suffixes such as 'st' or 'th' after the day (i.e. do not write *4th March*).

The body of the letter of transmittal should generally take the form of a 'good or neutral news' letter (although in some cases a 'bad news' letter may be appropriate); that is, it should contain:

- *a positive opening* — usually a straightforward statement indicating that the report is enclosed

- *further explanation* — generally includes a brief overview of the report, as well as brief details of the conclusions reached. Acknowledgement of any people who assisted in the report's preparation may be included here

- *a goodwill message* — a courteous closing in which you indicate what has to be done next, express your pleasure at being able to provide the information in the report and state your willingness to discuss the report in person. Refer to the example in Figure 3.1.

3.2.3 Title page

The title page is placed after the cover sheet and letter of transmittal and should provide the following:

- the title of the report, or restatement of assignment or essay question, usually also indicating the question number if a choice is given

- the name of the person for whom the report was prepared (instructor or client); sometimes the tutorial group or tutor's name is also required

- the date of submission of the report

- the student's name.

See Figure 3.2 for an example of a title page.

A REPORT ON THE OPERATIONS OF

AUSTRALIAN McDONALD'S STORES, 2001

Prepared for:

Dr. A. J. BLOGGS

Submitted: 10 March, 2001

Prepared by: A. J. STUDENT

B. F. GRADUATE

R. U. CURIOUS

FIGURE 3.2   Example of an assignment title page

3.2.4 Executive summary

The executive summary provides the reader with the report's major purpose, the analytical processes, the findings and the recommendations. It is so called because executives traditionally do not have sufficient time to read complete reports, and yet they need to extract sufficient information to make informed decisions. The executive summary should encourage the reader to go on to read the full report. It can also serve as a quick reference for the writer of the report at some future stage.

The executive summary is an extremely important component of any formal report and should be prepared *carefully*, rather than as an afterthought. Several drafts will be necessary to get it 'right'.

The executive summary will rarely be more than one page in length, and should not contain subheadings, direct quotes or unnecessary descriptive information. It should also be single-line spaced. It should contain a brief statement of the following:

- the purpose (objectives) and scope of the report

- the type of analysis conducted (and methods used)

- the most important and significant findings, in summary form

- the most important and significant recommendations.

It should be a 'stand-alone' document that encompasses the important points of the report it accompanies. Table 3.1 provides a guide to the approximate length of the executive summary.

TABLE 3.1	A guide to the length of an executive summary
REPORT LENGTH (WORDS)	**EXECUTIVE SUMMARY LENGTH (WORDS)**
1500	200–300
2000	250–350
3000	450–550

Note: The word count of the report *does not* include the executive summary, letter of transmittal, table of contents, figures, tables, references or appendices.

Most people recommend that the executive summary be written last, after the rest of the report has been prepared. This does not mean that it appears last in the report. It simply recognises that once the report is completed, and the conclusions and recommendations have been made, it is far easier to write an overall summary.

The executive summary should be given a page number using the lower-case roman numeral 'i' (if it runs to a second page, this should be marked with a 'ii'). Remember also that the executive summary *must* appear *before* the table of contents.

3.2.5 Table of contents

The table of contents should be listed on a new page of the report and, as for the executive summary, this page is numbered using a roman numeral (e.g. 'ii'). Sections are listed in the order in which they appear in the report, and the corresponding page numbers should be shown. Page 1 of the report, usually the introduction, follows the table of contents, and all subsequent sections are then numbered sequentially using arabic numerals (2, 3, 4 etc.).

When setting out your table of contents, the main section numbers should appear against the left-hand margin. There should then be one tab space to the heading of that section. Corresponding subsection numbers should appear indented one tab space from the left-hand margin, or under the first letter of the main heading, and subsection headings indented a further tab space to the right. Dot leaders may be used between the entry and page number to improve the clarity of the document. There are generally single spaces between subsections and double spaces between sections (see Figure 3.3).

TABLE OF CONTENTS	Page
Executive Summary	i
1. Introduction	1
1.1 Authorisation	1
1.2 Limitations	1
1.3 Scope of the report	2
2. The Current Situation	2
2.1 Basis for operations	3
2.1.1 Organisational structure	5
2.1.2 Operations code	6
2.2 Sales department	7
3. Planned Development	8
3.1 Objectives of the company	9
3.1.1 Assumptions	9
3.2 Priorities in implementing the plans	10
4. Conclusions	11
5. Recommendations	11
List of References	12
Appendices	
Appendix 1 — The organisational chart	13
Appendix 2 — Competitor analysis	14
List of tables	
Table 1 — The financial structure	6
ii	

FIGURE 3.3 Sample table of contents

If a section covers more than one page, only the page number on which the section begins need be shown in the table of contents.

Note: If submitting a report with a computer-generated table of contents, the formatting guideline outlined here might not strictly apply. Compare the table of contents at the front of this handbook, generated by computer, with the manually constructed one shown in Figure 3.3. Care should be taken to follow the example shown in Figure 3.3 as closely as possible.

Sub-subsections should be treated in a similar fashion — that is, two tab spaces from the left-hand margin, or under the first letter of the subheading title. Again, refer to the example provided in Figure 3.3. It is essential that all major headings and subheadings be clearly identifiable.

All appendices should be listed with their titles and corresponding page numbers. Following this, tables, then figures and then graphs should also be listed separately with their titles and corresponding page numbers. See Section 1.3.3 for differences between tables and figures.

3.2.6 Introduction

The introduction has three parts:

- the authorisation and purpose of the report — the reader must be told who commissioned the work and why the report was produced
- any limitations encountered in the production of the report that affected the results or the ability of the writer to complete the report
- the scope of the report — summarise what the report covers, how information is presented in the report, where the information for the report came from and how it was gathered (e.g. questionnaires or other research). Be careful here not to simply reproduce the table of contents — this should be an overview or summary of what was done, not a bit-by-bit reproduction. Focus on the important elements.

3.2.7 Body

This is the main part of the report and contains the discussions and analysis. The information in this section should be presented in a logical sequence, using paragraphing to separate ideas. As a general rule each paragraph should contain one main idea. Headings and subheadings should be used to identify each section and introduce new ideas or directions.

It is *very important* in this section to ensure that theoretical evidence or research findings are used to support the discussion. Throughout the report, answers should be provided to the following questions:

- How is this known?
- Why is this so?
- Why was this option selected? and
- Why was this course of action or design selected?

3.2.8 Conclusions

This section should essentially summarise the main points or findings of the assignment. It should be based on the information presented in the body. No new information should be introduced at this point, and the use of direct quotations should be avoided. The conclusion should answer the question: What do the findings mean?

It is important to ensure that your conclusions are consistent with the outline given in the introduction. For this reason, it is generally recommended that the introduction be written after the main report. The conclusion should answer the following questions:

- Was the purpose of the report fulfilled?

- Have the specified sources of information been used?

- Have the areas stated been adequately addressed?

3.2.9 Recommendations

Recommendations should be presented only when asked for. They are based on the conclusions and are the suggested options for solving the problem(s) that made writing the report necessary. Recommendations should be brief statements outlining a specific course of action suggested by your research — for example, 'That library hours be extended to 11.00 pm on week nights'.

It should be clearly demonstrated that detailed thought has been given to how the recommendations should be *implemented*, as well as what the resource *implications* might be for these. Consider the following questions:

- Are the recommendations *realistic* in the light of current environmental conditions (economic times, likely competitor reaction, government policy and consumer reactions)?

- Has sufficient thought been given to *timing and priorities*? When do the recommendations need to be implemented and in what order?

- Are the proposals *feasible*? Are there the financial, physical and human resources to support them?

3.2.10 Bibliography/List of references

Remember, a *list of references* is an alphabetical listing of any material actually *cited* in the report. A *bibliography* is an alphabetical listing of all the sources of information that have been read, used or referenced in researching and preparing the report. A bibliography will therefore contain any additional information that was reviewed in compiling the report, whether or not it was specifically cited.

While a formal report may require the inclusion of both, generally *only a list of references is demanded in student assignments*.

3.2.11 Glossary

A glossary is required only if a considerable number of technical terms have been used in the report and these may need to be explained to the reader. It is a form of mini-dictionary. It should start on a separate page. The term to be explained should be entered on the left and a definition, or reference, added on the right. For an example, refer to the glossary on page 93 of this handbook.

Be sure to reference correctly any definitions that have been taken from another author's work.

3.2.12 Appendices

Appendices generally contain:

- material that is too bulky to include in the body of the report

- material that is essential to explain a point but, if included in the body of the report, would distract the reader from the main message.

All appendices should be numbered sequentially (i.e. 1, 2, 3 etc.) and given a title. It is essential that direct reference be made in the main body of the report to each appendix. This will enable the reader to understand the material presented in the appendix in the context of the report.

Each appendix should begin on a new page, and each should usually contain only one major piece of information. However, if you have a number of tables, figures or graphs in which the information is interrelated, then an appendix can contain more than one piece of information. There is no limit to the number of appendices you can have (providing they are relevant).

Appendices usually include questionnaires, charts, maps, tables, extracts and so on. *It is very important that any material included in appendices is referenced correctly.* For example, if using a diagram from a textbook, there must be a reference for the source of that diagram.

3.3 Summary

A report is a special type of written communication used to provide concise information, and in some cases opinions, on a specific subject. Reports should be structured so that readers are guided through the main points. All relevant information should be included so that, after reading the report, readers will have a clear understanding of the key issues concerned.

Although most reports follow a fairly standard format, report layout may vary depending on the intended audience. Formal reports should include an assignment cover sheet, title page, letter of transmittal, executive summary, table of contents, introduction, the main body of the report, conclusions, recommendations, list of references, glossary (if required) and appendices.

Each of these components has been discussed in detail in this chapter.

The case study

4 The case study[3]

4.1 Introduction

A *case study* is a written description of a business problem or situation at a specific moment in time — it may be described as 'a snapshot in time'. A *case study analysis* is the critical review of that case information in combination with other secondary data in order to identify the problems or issues that are (or should be) important to that organisation. A formal *case report* is the written presentation of the analysis conducted, and demonstrates your understanding of the problems from both a theoretical and a practical perspective. The case report recommends solutions for those problems based on a theoretical framework. Some courses may ask for a less formal style of case report; however, the appropriate methods of analysis remain the same. You need to check your assignment overview to establish the style of report required for your unit.

Sometimes the organisation on which the case was based will be disguised. Usually, however, the actual organisation name and names of the people in that organisation are used. Cases include important information that has a bearing on the issues central to the case analysis. However, seemingly irrelevant pieces of information (called 'red herrings') are sometimes included to give a more rounded picture of the organisation, and the general environment, at the time of writing.

You will encounter much variation from course to course on what is called a 'case study'. The Harvard MBA case study format is used mainly in advanced subjects and postgraduate courses, and usually demands a detailed and lengthy discussion about an organisation. This style of case study requires students to analyse the problem(s) and ultimately provide decision recommendations and implementation plans.

Another type of case study that students will encounter is a short (1–3 pages), less formal description of an organisation or business situation. Questions that require students to apply theoretical arguments and/or analytical skills in their answers are often attached to this form of case study. Some lecturers may also use the term 'case study' when they require students to give practical examples or to describe scenarios.

Whichever form you encounter, case studies are designed to provide students with opportunities to experience the challenges faced in real-life situations. The main objectives of any case study are:

- to assist students in learning to apply various theories through simulated problem-solving and decision-making

---

3. We gratefully acknowledge contribution to this section by Mr Cec Pederson.

- to allow students to learn by ***doing*** through the application of principles, rather than through passive learning forms such as listening to lecturers and reading textbooks

- to allow students to reinforce and apply theories and concepts in managerial contexts.

The information contained in this chapter is based on the longer Harvard case study format. However, it can be applied generally to each of the case study formats mentioned previously.

Given the variety of ways in which case studies are used, you may be given specific instructions by your instructor about how to structure your case report. These directions may differ in detail from the information contained in this chapter. Check your course instructions for this. However, if no specific information is provided, use the format presented here.

4.2 Preparing a case analysis

The case analysis technique requires a great deal of creativity, but this gets easier with practice (Kashani 1993). It is important to recognise that there is no ***one*** correct solution to a case study. There may be a number of feasible strategies that management could adopt, each having different implications for the future of the company and involving different trade-offs. A good case analysis will allow students, drawing on the data gathered and on the relevant theory, to put forward a report that has recommendations based on strong, well-presented and -supported arguments (Lovelock 1992).

Just as there is no single correct answer in case analysis, there is also no one 'best way' to complete the analysis. However, a number of generally recommended procedures will help students to achieve a satisfactory result. Often, the major problem for students when faced with a case study is 'Where do I begin?'. The following advice should help to overcome that problem:

- ***Read*** the case through once ***without*** taking any notes or highlighting points of interest or importance.

- ***Leave*** the case for at least 24 hours. During that time, review your textbooks or study notes for the theoretical implications of the material contained in the case. This may help you to identify the problems or issues more clearly in the next stages of the analysis process. It will also help to keep you focused on the relevant theoretical framework.

- ***Re-read*** the case, this time making notes and highlighting areas that seem important or inconsistent with the general direction of the material. At this stage you are really only 'fishing' — looking for anything that stands out. This is often a good time to manipulate the data in any financial tables — to calculate ratios, percentage increases/decreases and differences between years, for example. This will often form the basis for your analysis. Do not attempt to formulate too many answers at this point. You are looking only for trends, inconsistencies and a general overview of the company and the situation.

- *Organise* the information you have noted. See if you can identify any potential problems for the company and the possible reasons for those problems. Identify any areas about which you need more information, perhaps utilising other sources such as textbooks, journals, newspapers and the business press. You might ask yourself the following questions:

    - What sort of organisation does the case concern?

    - What is the nature of the industry (broadly defined)?

    - What is going on in the external environment?

    - What issues do management seem to be facing?

    - How can any tables or figures provided be used to further the analysis?

    - Can new insights be gained by combining or recalculating data presented in the case (e.g. using ratios or percentages)?

    - What is really happening in this situation? Quite often you will need to 'read between the lines' in order to better understand the issues. Do not take as fact the perspective, hints and biases the case writer or the management of the company is giving (Kashani 1993).

- One way to help you make sense at this stage of the information you are compiling is to use strategic analysis tools such as a *situation analysis* and/or a *SWOT analysis*. These tools will provide a framework within which you can organise and clarify relevant information and the relationships that may exist between issues. Section 4.4 discusses both of these techniques in detail. Some courses will require these tools to be used; others will not. Indeed, such tools may be totally inappropriate for some case studies, especially the shorter versions with questions attached. It is a good idea to check your course instructions for more information about what is required in this area.

- Begin to gather more general information about the company, or about the industry within which this organisation operates. This background information will help you to better understand the context of the problems and possible industry trends. You may also need to be aware of the external environment at the time of the case; for example, what was the economy doing, and what were the social norms?

- Begin drafting your report using the headings and components discussed in the next section (see Chapters 1 and 2 for more information on the writing style and referencing format required). Before you start this stage, ensure you have spent sufficient time on the analysis. Do not be tempted to arrive at a quick solution. It is also very important not to identify with the organisation in the case. You should adopt a third-person view about what you believe it should or should not do. So avoid sentences that begin, 'We should …' Remember, too, that you should beware of being misled by management's own views of what the issues are.

- *Discuss your results when you reach the first draft stage.* Get together with a small group of your fellow students (preferably those who you know are at a similar stage in the project) and discuss your findings and, most important, your recommendations and reasoning. This allows you to check that you have thought things through and have not overlooked any vital information. It is important that you do not use this session to 'check' your answers. Rather, it is an opportunity to revise your arguments in the light of different perspectives. Do not worry if your answers differ from those of your friends. You may have used different reference material or approached the problem differently.

- *Polish* your report, proofread for spelling, typos and grammatical errors. Double-check all referencing and ensure that all appendices are attached.

4.3 The structure of the case analysis report

When presenting your results, the case report format varies slightly from a traditional report format (see Section 3.1). Generally, in a case study you are given detailed information about an organisation or situation, and you are required to analyse this information, to identify the problems correctly, to demonstrate an understanding of the causes and effects of the problems, and to provide recommended solutions based on a theoretical framework.

A formal case report generally has the following sections:

1. Assignment cover page
2. Letter of transmittal (not always required)
3. Title page
4. Executive summary
5. Table of contents
6. Introduction or case background
7. Body of the analysis, which includes the following subheadings:
   (i) Problem identification or identification of case issues
   (ii) Problem analysis and justification
8. Alternative solutions
9. Recommendation(s)
10. Implementation plan (if requested)
11. List of references
12. Appendices

You will note that this format differs somewhat from the report style discussed in Chapter 3. As points 1 to 5 are discussed thoroughly in that chapter, they will not be reviewed here. Rather, points 6 to 11 (which either are not addressed or have requirements that differ from those covered in Chapter 3) will be discussed in more detail with the aid of the following example (McArthur 1997).

A sample case scenario

Marilyn White was a meticulous and detail-minded employee who was promoted to a supervisory position almost a year ago. Over the past few months there have been problems within Marilyn's department. Marilyn allows no initiative on the part of her employees. She insists on checking every piece of work that leaves the department, with the result that her subordinates spend large amounts of time waiting for her to check their work, or redoing work that does not meet her exacting standards. Consequently, productivity is low. Staff morale is poor, a number of members having left the organisation or being on the point of leaving. Marilyn herself is increasingly stressed. What can be done about Marilyn?

4.3.1 Introduction or case background

This section should provide a short summary of the current background of the case and should lead to the issues confronting management. This section should be *no longer than one-third to half a page*. It should 'set the scene' for your analysis.

One way to begin organising your thoughts for this part of the process is to list what you see as the main points in the case. For example, the main ideas from the scenario above are shown in Figure 4.1. You will need to summarise these points to write your introduction.

- Marilyn was recently promoted to supervisor based upon attributes of meticulousness and attention to detail.

- Marilyn's supervisory behaviour can be characterised as:
  — allowing no initiative from employees
  — insisting on checking all work against her exacting standards; and
  — ordering work not up to her standards to be redone.

- Employees have idle time because they have to wait for Marilyn to check their work.

- Employees have to spend double the time on a job they have to redo to meet Marilyn's standards.

- Productivity is low.

- Staff morale is low, partly because of loss, and pending loss, of staff from her department.

- Marilyn is increasingly stressed.

FIGURE 4.1   An example of a list of main points

4.3.2 Body of the analysis

In this section you are required to list briefly the main issues or problems in the case and then to discuss why they are problems with reference to the appropriate theory and examples. The two parts to this section are:

- *problem identification,* sometimes referred to as *identification of case issues* (check your course instructions for required terminology)

- *problem analysis and justification.*

These subsections will now be discussed.

1. Problem identification or identification of case issues

Some issues you identify may not be problems as such. Rather, a number of issues may need to be addressed before they *become* problems, or perhaps there are opportunities that have not been identified effectively and/or exploited. Whether they are issues or problems, it is important that they be identified clearly and precisely and, when there is more than one, that they be prioritised.

It is also important to define the case problems or issues in terms of the specific concepts or relevant theories you are studying. If the course is Consumer Behaviour, use consumer behaviour terminology or theory, not general marketing theory, in your statement of issues. Similarly, if it is an Industrial Relations unit, apply that theory and not general human resources theory. Your instructor will want you to focus on the issues relevant to the particular subject. This approach will also allow you to communicate better and to focus on solutions relevant to the issues you have identified.

A case study is often built around several interrelated problems or issues. In order to make sense of these, and to organise them usefully, you need to adopt a systematic and logical approach that will enable you to get to the heart of the problem. Often, the problem or issues may not be evident and you will have to sift through the information, teasing out particulars that are *symptoms* related to the problem itself. As you identify the symptoms, you will be building up evidence that will point to the major cause or underlying *problem.* Remember to look closely at the information in the introduction. It is most important at this stage that you do not stray from the actual evidence contained in the case.

Of each symptom, ask the question *What caused this?* and note your answers. You may find that you can then ask the question again, and this time the chances are high that you will reach the source of the problem or issue. When you have finished listing the symptoms and no longer have anything of which you can ask *What caused this?,* you should be able to identify the problem or issues. Table 4.1 presents an example of this process applied to the example scenario. In this case, the problem is evident — it is Marilyn's supervisory style. You can see in this example that if you were to list all the items categorised here as symptoms, you would not really be getting to the heart of the problem, and you would not achieve maximum marks.

TABLE 4.1	Example of problem identification process	
SYMPTOM	**WHAT CAUSED THE SYMPTOM?**	**AND WHAT CAUSED THIS?**
Low productivity	Marilyn's insistence on checking all work Marilyn's insistence on staff redoing work not up to her exacting standards	Marilyn's supervisory style
Low staff morale	Staff spend idle time waiting for Marilyn. Staff have to redo work, doubling the time necessary to produce the product. Staff initiative not permitted.	Marilyn's supervisory style
Staff turnover increasing	Staff initiative not permitted. Staff spend too much time idle, waiting for Marilyn to check finished work.	Marilyn's supervisory style

In this situation you would state that the main problem is Marilyn's supervisory style, as evidenced by the low productivity of her staff, their low morale and the high staff turnover.

2. Problem analysis and justification

Now that you have identified the problem, this section answers the question: *Why are they problems?* To achieve this, you need to:

- identify the underlying causes of the problems

- justify why they are problems by using supporting concepts, frameworks and other material from your course of study

- examine the effects of the problems on the organisation.

Here you can start to hypothesise (to guess in an informed way using logic and problem-solving techniques such as brain-storming) the factors that have brought about these problems or issues. This is where you should consider the relevant theories and/or theoretical issues that relate to the situation. You will need to have theoretical support and demonstrate evidence of wide reading by including referenced content from other authors. Remember, you will enhance considerably both your analysis and your final grade if you can demonstrate an understanding of the theoretical concepts from the relevant course of study by applying these to the case.

You will also need to demonstrate, through your discussion, that you have an understanding of the organisation, the industry and the external environment.

You should use this section to explore the options available to the organisation, and to identify and develop the theoretical implications of these options. Figure 4.2 gives an example of the issues that might be explored from the sample scenario. Answers to each of the questions posed at this stage will also lead in the direction of *possible* solutions.

In the scenario given, you might well raise the following questions:

- Which of the company's selection procedures has resulted in the selection of a person on criteria other than those that we might expect to be important in a supervisor (e.g. leadership style)? Are there any theories that would support or explain this?

- Why has there not been an improvement in the quality of output by the workforce as the 'new' standards are recognised? What are the relationships between Marilyn and the rest of her workers? Why are they not responding positively? What does the theory say about this? Is it a common occurrence? Why? Why not? What solutions does the theory propose for this?

- Has Marilyn been given supervisory training? What kinds of training does the theory say she should have had, when and why?

- Has Marilyn been mentored in her job? What does the theory on mentoring say about this?

- What is the culture of the organisation? What does the theory say about the role of organisational culture in supervision, and is it relevant or helpful in explaining what has happened here?

- What was Marilyn's predecessor's style? What does the theory say about this as a factor, and how is it important in this analysis and the search for solutions?

FIGURE 4.2 Example of problem analysis process

4.3.3 Formulation of alternatives or possible solutions

Before recommending a course of action, you must examine alternative ways that the problem(s) or issue(s) can be solved or resolved. It is important that a range of alternative courses of action is fully evaluated before one or more are ultimately selected (Kashani 1993). Remember that there is more than one solution to most management issues.

This section, then, answers the question *What are the options?* It should also explain in some detail why the proposed alternatives are appropriate. The question to be asked of each alternative is, *If this is done, or not done, then what?* It is important to remember that the alternatives you suggest should be consistent with the environment in which the firm is operating, be persuasive in their promise to solve the problem and, ultimately, be implementable. You may also need to think of alternatives in terms of short-term tactics and long-term strategies.

A good starting point is to list the alternatives in point form. Alternatives may not be mutually exclusive. A combination of actions may be appropriate. Each alternative should be explored in terms of its feasibility and the potential consequences of its adoption. In the case of the sample scenario, the list of possible alternatives might resemble that in Figure 4.3.

1.	Do nothing.
2.	Fire/sack/dismiss Marilyn.
3.	Transfer Marilyn.
4.	Counsel Marilyn for stress and leadership style.
5.	Train Marilyn.
6.	Mentor Marilyn.
7.	Give team training to the whole department.
8.	Check management policy regarding selection, supervisor manual and mentoring.
9.	Train management in quality service techniques, teamwork and empowerment.

FIGURE 4.3 List of alternative actions

When making *What if* judgements, or decisions about the advantages and disadvantages of alternative actions and combinations of actions, you should use the main issues or problems that have been identified in the first section as a framework for evaluation. Remember that, ultimately, the proposed solutions need to resolve the issues or problems, so their relative merits should be considered in those terms. In many case studies there is a need to solve immediate issues or problems and then to advise medium- to longer-term strategies. In our scenario, time is very much a factor. Something should be done ***now***. Such a factor should not, however, limit adoption of a wider view. See Table 4.2 for examples of analysis of the alternatives for the sample scenario. Take each of the possible solutions and evaluate it in point form to build up a framework for the discussion in your report.

Three last points on the formulation and evaluation of alternatives:

1　When preparing action alternatives, do not discard any option without first evaluating it at some length.

2　Before finalising your suggestions, try to think through the mechanics of how they are supposed to work. Ask yourself, 'What are the critical steps and how will they help solve the main issues or problems identified?'.

3　Once you have chosen which option or combination of options to adopt, think about possible criticisms the plan might encounter. This advance mental preparation will help you to develop a more persuasive argument to support the course of action you have chosen.

TABLE 4.2	Evaluating alternative actions	
	POSSIBLE SOLUTION	**THEN WHAT?**
1.	Do nothing.	▪ problem persists (and might get worse) ▪ increased loss of productivity and increased costs
2.	Fire/sack/dismiss Marilyn.	▪ loss of an asset ▪ replacement cost ▪ unless new criteria for selection are used, another Marilyn might emerge
3.	Transfer Marilyn.	▪ loss of an asset ▪ could still cause same problem in a new place ▪ still have to find a suitable replacement
4.	Counsel Marilyn for stress and leadership style.	▪ should work, OK for immediate solution, but must be complemented by other actions
5.	Train Marilyn.	▪ weigh up cost vs benefit ▪ could increase her asset worth
6.	Mentor Marilyn.	▪ weigh up cost vs benefit ▪ need to find a suitable person ▪ gains to be made in the long term
7.	Introduce team training.	▪ potential for great benefit ▪ cost and loss of some productivity in short term, but gains to be made in long term
8.	Review management policies.	▪ assistance needed (consultant) ▪ cost ▪ benefits in medium and long term
9.	Train management in quality processes.	▪ will have the ability to model new practice ▪ potential benefits from empowerment

4.3.4 Recommendations or choice of solutions

This section of your report will answer the question *What should be done?* It should be based on the previous section's analysis and should be relatively brief, since the discussion of the advantages of the proposed solutions was covered in the previous section, where the alternatives were evaluated. Depending on the type of case and the number of issues or problems identified, a number of recommendations may be made in this section. Recommendations should be prioritised, and there should be a very brief reiteration of the main reasons these options should be chosen. You may wish to subdivide this section into short-term and long-term solutions. See Figure 4.4 for examples of recommendations that might be applied to the sample scenario.

From consideration of the options proposed in Table 4.2, it is suggested that the firm adopt options 4, 5, 6, 7, 8 and 9.

The most important course of action — which should be implemented immediately — is to counsel Marilyn about her leadership style and to give her appropriate mentoring. As soon as possible after this she should also be given some directed supervisory training. In recognition of the difficulties under which Marilyn's team has been working, it is also important that the work group receive assistance. Some form of intervention is necessary and it is suggested that the use of a consultant to study group dynamics with them could help overcome their problems and get them working well together.

In the short and medium terms, the advantages of management's adopting and being trained in Quality Service processes should be given serious consideration. The benefits that would accrue from such a strategy would help minimise the chances of this situation recurring.

FIGURE 4.4 Recommendations

4.3.5 Implementation plan

Your recommendations will not be complete unless you give some thought to how your proposed strategy should be implemented. Therefore, the implementation details must be presented. The implementation plan should also provide persuasive evidence for gaining acceptance of the recommendations, because it indicates that the recommendations are feasible and practical.

This section, then, answers the questions *Who will do it, how will it be done and when?* To answer these questions you will need to consider the issues of:

- *resources* (physical, financial and human)
- *timing and sequencing* (When and in what order should things be done?)
- *responsibility* (Who is responsible for ensuring that it happens?)
- *measurement* (How will the success, or otherwise, of this recommendation be measured?)
- *possible impacts from the external environment* (Will the competition react to this proposal and how will that affect its success? Similarly, how will the government react, if at all, and are there any legal ramifications of the proposal?).

This section needs to be convincingly argued, both to the organisation depicted in the case study and to the marker. Figure 4.5 itemises some of the implementation issues that need to be considered from the sample scenario. **Note:** These are in point form only; in *your* case report they should be expanded and discussed fully.

Spend time ensuring the quality of your case write-ups. Allow at least 3–4 weeks, if possible. It is very obvious to the marker if you have not spent time on your analysis. Last-minute, all-night efforts will be destined to failure!

- Arrange for Marilyn to be
  - (a) counselled for stress
  - (b) counselled for her leadership style
  - (c) given immediate mentoring support.

The costs of these counselling programs are likely to be less than those involving recruitment and selection of a new staff member. If Marilyn will not agree, point out the alternatives, with loss of her employment as one option.

- Arrange for a consultant to assist the work group using group dynamics.
- Prepare position paper on the benefits to management of Quality Service processes.
- Include project timeline and costs. Estimate the benefits to the company.

FIGURE 4.5 Implementation

Think in terms of a highly paid, busy senior executive reading this report. You need to get your arguments across forcefully and not waste time setting the scene or transmitting information the reader already knows or that has little or no relevance to the problems identified. This reader probably would not want to spend much time flipping through appendices, so the body of your report will need to stand alone. It is also likely that in the 'real world' this busy executive would engage other analysts to carefully examine your calculations and appendices, so make sure they are accurate and well prepared.

As you can see, the case analysis process requires you to anchor the case in time and identify critical points that enable you to analyse and filter the information towards achieving a set of recommendations and a viable implementation plan. So there needs to be a clear thread from the start of the case report to the end, where your recommendations and implementation plans are logically related to your problems and analysis.

4.4 Strategic analysis tools

Section 4.2 mentioned two strategic analysis tools that can greatly assist your case study preparation: the situation analysis and the SWOT analysis. Although these are optional tools, some courses require the use of one, or both, as evidence in the analysis. Check your course guidelines to see if these tools are specific requirements for the case analysis you are conducting. These tools will now be discussed in more detail.

4.4.1 The SWOT analysis

A SWOT analysis requires you to identify the firm's strengths and weaknesses, as well as the external environmental opportunities and threats (see Figure 4.6). If you *do* make use of either a situation analysis or a SWOT analysis, make sure you include the results in an appendix to the final report as supporting information.

Strengths	Weaknesses	Opportunities	Threats
✓	✓	✓	✓
✓	✓	✓	✓
✓	✓	✓	✓
✓	✓	✓	✓

FIGURE 4.6 SWOT analysis

4.4.2 Situation analysis

A situation analysis is not an essential item for case analysis, but many students find it a helpful tool. Figure 4.7 shows the situational analysis framework (Payne 1993). You will note that not all the analysis areas suggested will be relevant to every discipline area, and indeed there may be other areas that are important for a particular case. The situation analysis is therefore open to modification. Its main use is to help students make sense of the relationships between areas of importance and to ensure that all areas have been given due consideration.

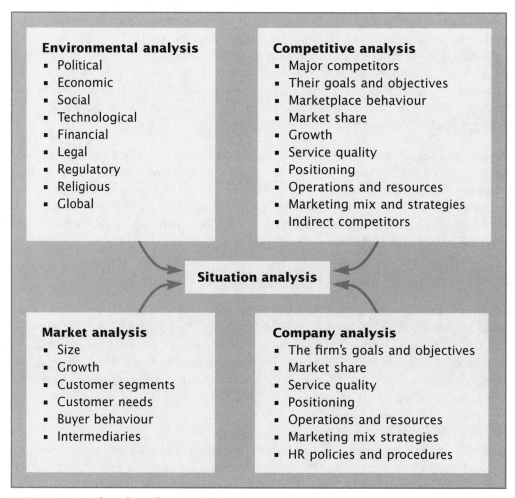

FIGURE 4.7 The situation analysis

4.5 Summary

There are two main types of case study that students may encounter. They are:

- the short case study

- the Harvard MBA style case study.

The short case study normally consists of a short description of an organisation or business situation. This type of case study may be used by instructors to provide examples to demonstrate how particular theoretical concepts apply in practical situations. Questions that require students to apply theoretical and analytical skills to provide an answer may also be attached to a case study of this type.

For the longer Harvard MBA style case study, a more detailed case analysis and subsequent report is generally required.

Remember that most case reports have drawn on a considerable quantity of research material for their analysis and to develop their recommendations. This material should be placed in an appendix in order to streamline the report and to reduce the word length. Remember, though, that you will need to refer to the material in the appendices in the body of the report, and you will also need to summarise the main points or findings of such material, not just refer the marker to a particular appendix.

 Based on the results of the strategic analysis, it can be seen that a diversification strategy will provide Smith Chemicals with the best outcome. This strategy was particularly evident following the identification of the company's weak financial status, combined with increasingly aggressive competition from a number of key players in the industry, and a general decline in market share (see the complete strategic analysis in Appendix 3 for more specific details).

Not this:

Based on the results of the strategic analysis (Appendix 3), it can be seen that a diversification strategy will provide Smith Chemicals with the best outcome.

In this chapter the steps required to prepare a Harvard MBA style case study and the components required in the resulting case study report were discussed in detail. Examples of case analysis techniques and sample report sections were also provided.

4.6 List of references

Lovelock, CH 1991, *Services marketing*, 2nd edn, Prentice Hall, Englewood Cliffs, New Jersey.

Kashani, K 1992, *Managing global marketing*, PWS Kent, USA.

Essay writing

5 Essay writing

5.1 Introduction

During your studies at university you may be required to write numerous formal essays. This experience will help you to acquire written communication skills that are essential in many careers. Since they require you to weigh up conflicting evidence in order to reach a conclusion, essay writing will also help you to develop reasoning skills. In order to find appropriate reference material, sound library research skills, which will benefit you over the long term, must also be developed. Essays differ from reports in a number of ways. Specifically, they require a different format or layout, and also a different style of writing. An essay requires the writer to argue, defend or justify a point or view with respect to a particular topic or question. To this end, essays require cohesive arguments couched in complete and well-considered sentences and paragraphs. Dot (bullet) points and short annotated sentences should be avoided.

There are a number of steps to writing a formal essay. The key stages are explored in the following section.

5.2 Selecting the topic

The first step is to select a topic (if given a choice). It is a good idea to be guided in your selection by personal interest, but availability of library and other resources should also be taken into account.

5.3 Analysing the topic

Once you have selected the topic, make sure of the essay question's require-ments. Look up any unfamiliar words in a dictionary. If the question is based on a term that is contested (that is, where there is no consensus on a definition), there might be a need to incorporate in the essay some discussion about the definition. For example, if required to 'discuss whether or not Australia is a democracy', your answer would depend very much on how 'democracy' was defined.

Note also what action the instruction verb requires. For example, 'discuss' requires a different style of writing from 'debate'. The glossary on page 93 out-lines some of the more common instruction verbs used in various forms of assessment.

Note any qualifying words or phrases that set limits to your study. If you were asked to 'evaluate the claim that throughout the 1990s Australian unionism was under siege', you would need to concentrate on a particular location (Australia) during a particular era (the 1990s).

Remember, there is no *one* correct answer to an essay question. Generally, there are many explanations about why things occur, and many solutions to particular problems; you will need to weigh up the evidence presented for each point of view. Even if you are convinced that a particular position is correct, it is essential to acknowledge opposing arguments and indicate what you perceive to be their failings.

5.4 Planning

Once you are sure you know what the question is asking you to do, you can begin planning the essay. This is not an easy task, because it is difficult to initiate a plan without knowing much about the topic. Some initial reading may be needed in order for you to begin formulating ideas. Once the topic has been grasped, the planning can commence. This is an important stage, because the plan ensures the material is arranged in a logical way. While a plan is essential, it is also important to recognise that this structure is not fixed rigidly at this stage. Subsequent research may introduce new ideas that need to be incorporated in the original plan.

5.5 Research

You will normally be expected to go beyond the study material provided and the textbook in order to find sufficient material for an essay. Wide reading will provide sufficient breadth of knowledge to make judgements about conflicting points of view.

The course instructor will generally provide written guidelines about suitable texts.

Reference lists in relevant books are also useful, as is the library subject index. Librarians are generally willing to help students to find appropriate material (see Section 1.5.3). Do not leave your research to the last minute, as you might find the material you want has already been borrowed.

Once suitable reference sources have been found, the necessary information should be noted or photocopies made of the relevant material. The reference material used should be organised or filed in some fashion, especially if the essay is a long one. Make sure detailed records of all relevant reference material are kept so that material can be correctly cited.

 'Post-it' notes are very useful for marking pages of books from which citations will be made. Manila folders, labelled according to theme or topic, are a simple and useful method for organising and storing reference material for long essays or reports.

5.6 Writing the essay

Once the material has been gathered, the writing can begin. An essay must have an *introduction*, a *body* and a *conclusion*. The introduction should tell the reader what to expect. Essays are not mystery stories, where the reader waits until the end to find out what it has all been about. The introduction should introduce the main theme or argument so that the reader has some idea of what follows. You might find it useful to write the introduction last. You can then ensure it is consistent with the arguments and evidence presented in your essay.

Remember that the first part of each sentence, paragraph and essay has the most impact on the reader's mind, so always express your main idea (rather than parenthetical issues) at the start. For example, the first sentence of a paragraph should be a topic or theme sentence that summarises the main idea that will be developed in the paragraph. Each paragraph should contain one main idea. Avoid one-sentence paragraphs — academic ideas should be complex enough to warrant more than a single sentence to present them. Also avoid long, tortuous sentences that are hard to follow. Try to include a *linker* (e.g. 'Furthermore . . .', 'On the other hand . . .' or 'The next step is . . .') at the start of each paragraph so the reader can clearly follow your line of thought from paragraph to paragraph. A *summary sentence* at the end of the paragraph or section will also help to clarify your argument.

Your argument should be presented in the body of the essay and be supported by evidence. Make sure that what is written here is consistent with and does not contradict the points made in the introduction. Also, ensure that related ideas are grouped together in paragraphs, and that the final sentence of each provides a link to the next set of related ideas in the following paragraph.

The conclusion should tie together the themes discussed in the essay and spell out their implications. Make sure that the conclusion is consistent with the introduction and with what the question asks. Be aware, too, that the conclusion is not the place to introduce new ideas. These must appear in the body of the essay.

Students will usually be expected to write a number of drafts of an essay, a task made considerably easier by word processing technology. If possible, it is a good idea to put the essay aside for a day or two before completing the final draft. This allows a more objective assessment of both the arguments presented and the style of writing used.

5.7 Style

For an essay to be effective, ideas must be communicated clearly. If your first language is English you should already be familiar with the tools of communication. If you are having trouble with communication, you should seek help from your relevant university student services section. Communication skills can be improved by reading as much as possible. In this way, your vocabulary will improve and the patterns of the language will become more familiar.

For essay presentation, see the general guidelines for assessment, specifically Sections 1.1, 1.2 and 1.3.

Quotations should not be used to 'write' an essay. They may be used sparingly to support or *illustrate* points in the argument, not to make them. You must summarise the quotations themselves as well as formulate your interpretation of what they mean and how they add to or support your argument. Do not leave it to the reader to interpret their meaning or relevance.

As a general rule, headings are not used in formal essays; however, check with your instructor about whether headings are acceptable in the particular circumstances of your assignment. If this is not clearly spelt out, and you cannot reach your instructor, assume headings are not desirable.

Some people argue that headings are inappropriate in an essay, while others believe they are useful as signposts that guide the reader (and the writer) through the essay. If you do use headings, do not number them — and use them sparingly. Do not forget to write sentences that link each subsection with the next.

5.8 Sample essay

The following sample assignment question and essay will illustrate some of the main points made in this chapter. It is based on and, in part, extracted from an essay written by an MBA student.

The following assignment was set for Consumer Behaviour students:

> Observational learning is an important means of socialisation for children, teenagers and adults. Consider the content of popular prime-time television shows. What are the patterns of behaviour that people may learn as a result of watching prime-time television? What, if any, are the public policy implications of your analysis?

In response to this assignment question, some students wrote essays on the impact of observational learning on socialisation in which they examined the ethical and social issues involved in this area in relation to television programming. One student, Lisa, wrote an essay that was particularly well structured and written, and this is an adaptation of her work.

Note that this essay does not include headings, although in many cases this would be permissible. Check with your instructor and/or the assignment guidelines to determine the ruling on this for your particular assignment.

Observational learning and public policy implications

Observational learning, also known as vicarious or social learning, plays a significant role in the socialisation of individuals (Mowen & Minor 1998). The purpose of this paper is to address the theoretical issues related to observational learning as a mechanism that results in consumer socialisation. In particular, the scope of this paper will be confined to how people learn patterns of behaviour by observing others in prime-time television shows. A discussion of observational learning and the process of socialisation is presented, followed by a review of the patterns of behaviour that may be learned as a result of watching prime-time television shows. Finally, some implications for public policy in this area are presented.

Observational learning has been defined as 'the phenomenon whereby people develop patterns of behaviour by observing the actions of others' (Mowen & Minor 1998, p. 47). This theory identifies two ways in which people's behaviour can be affected. The first is where a person perceives positive consequences resulting from the observed behaviour; they are likely to imitate such behaviour. The second is where a person perceives negative consequences of an observed behaviour; they are likely to attempt to avoid such behaviour (Assael 1995). In this manner the theory of observational learning incorporates both the principles of cognitive learning, where people are anticipating consequences of actions, and the principles of operant conditioning — where reinforcement is shown to shape behaviour (Mowen & Minor 1998). It is these learning mechanisms that are known to contribute to the process of socialisation.

Socialisation is defined as 'the process by which individuals acquire the knowledge, skills and dispositions that enable them to participate as members of society' (Mowen & Minor 1998, p. 534). From a consumer behaviour perspective, socialisation refers to how people acquire skills, knowledge and attitudes that enable them to function as consumers in the marketplace (Assael 1995; Schiffman et al. 1997). Children, specifically, learn consumption skills as part of the socialisation process from interaction with family members, peers and the media, particularly the persuasive influence of television (Craig-Lees et al. 1995; Schiffman et al. 1997; Mowen & Minor 1998). Prime-time television, in particular, has the ability to influence much behaviour, both positively and negatively, due to its wide reach. Children are most vulnerable to this form of persuasion.

> Selection of her topic was important to Lisa. She chose to write about this topic from a range of topics because she was interested in it and was able to find suitable references.

> Lisa's introduction tells the reader how she has interpreted the topic and how the essay is structured. Now the reader knows what to expect.

> Note the strong link from this paragraph to the next. The reader is led into the paragraph expecting to read about children and persuasion.

It is well known that prior to a child developing abstract thought, which occurs at about the age of ten, they are particularly vulnerable to advertising messages and the seductive appeal of television reality (Craig-Lees et al. 1995; Schiffman et al. 1997; Mowen & Minor 1998). Children (and others) learn by observing the patterns and consequences of behaviours of television actors in simulated television realities and use these as guides for their own consumption and social behaviours. Prime-time television shows are well known for containing story-lines that include subtle product marketing messages, as well as behavioural modelling scenarios (Schiffman 1997). This has particular relevance for marketers in developing promotional strategies aimed at children in particular.

In spite of the obvious implications for observational learning in the socialisation of children, socialisation is an ongoing process and is not strictly confined to childhood, although it is more intense for those at an earlier age (Loudon & Della Bitta 1993). Teenagers and adults also are continually undergoing further socialisation as their reference groups, social settings and circumstances change. This means that there is potential to influence consumption behaviour through many stages of a person's life. Interestingly, in relation to consumption it is noted that observational learning through socialisation of the family has the greatest influence on the rational aspects of consumption, while learning through observation from television and the media influences the emotional aspects of consumption (Assael 1995).

> Each key idea that Lisa introduces is appropriately referenced.

The general patterns of behaviour that people learn from viewing prime-time television shows can be both positive and negative. Negative behaviours such as insolence, disrespect for elders. a dislike of learning and even aggression may come from shows such as 'South Park', 'The Simpsons', most sporting programs and even, to some degree, 'Neighbours' and 'Home and Away'. Positive behaviours such as helping, good parenting skills, caring for friends and telling the truth may come from shows like 'The Pretender', 'Blue Heelers', 'Home Improvements', 'Friends' and 'Seinfeld'. Television is a useful medium for developing desired modelling scenarios where people engage in certain behaviours and subsequently receive reinforcement (Loudon & Della Bitta 1993) — for example a sit-com which shows someone telling the truth about a transgression and instead of being punished, they are rewarded for their honesty. Television also has the ability to engage in product marketing at both an obvious level (shows such as 'Burke's Backyard' and 'Bright Ideas') and at a less obvious level (such as when the stars of 'Friends' go to a Hootie and the Blowfish concert) (Mowen & Minor 1998).

The effect of prime-time television shows engaging in product marketing has implications for public policy, particularly in relation to the impact on children. The greater the exposure children have to television, the greater the probability that they will accept the images and associations observed (Assael 1995; Shiffman et al. 1997). This is particularly critical when it is known that for the majority of children younger than nine years, television is their principal source of marketplace information (Craig-Lees et al. 1995). It is for this reason that many countries, including Australia, have begun to regulate the content and timing of television advertising and programming. In spite of this, recent research has suggested that parents and friends still have a greater influence over children's product choices than does television advertising, although the friends most likely get their information from television (O'Shannessy 1994; Moschis 1985; Childers & Akshay 1992).

Here Lisa is developing her argument and supporting her views with researched evidence.

This regulation of television content and advertising is both a government and an industry initiative through legislation and the Federation of Australian Commercial Television Stations (FACTS). There is also more advertising of the existence of such regulatory bodies and of the rights of television watchers in an attempt to better inform the marketplace and to empower them into becoming more involved consumers.

Consumers who are more aware of their rights are less likely to be subjected to unethical practices, which has been the criticism of many in relation to the use of product marketing on prime-time television (Mowen & Minor 1998). The complete embargo of the use of product marketing is not a feasible option for policy makers, so their best course of action is to focus on consumer education using the same principles of observational learning on their target audiences.

In summary, observational learning has been shown to be an important learning mechanism for the socialisation of consumers. It is directly through observation that many consumers learn the appropriate consumption behaviours and social norms of our society. Prime-time television shows provide viewers with access to 'real life' scenarios that consumers use to match and modify their own behaviours to, and in this regard they can be open to misuse by unethical marketers. Whether obvious or subtle, product marketing in television shows can add authenticity to a product because a consumer is less likely to discount the message, and this is particularly true in the case of young children (Mowen & Minor 1998). By understanding this socialisation process, public policy makers, through implementing both regulation and educational programs, are able to ensure that consumers are not unfairly or unethically treated by unscrupulous marketers.

In her conclusion, Lisa ties the points in her discussion together. She finishes with an interesting and supported statement that confirms her initial opening that observational learning helps in the development of public policy for advertising.

References

Assael, H 1995, *Consumer behaviour and marketing action*, 5th edn, South-Western College Publishing, Ohio.

Childers, TL and Akshay, RR 1992, 'The influence of familial and peer-based reference groups on consumer decisions', *Journal of Consumer Research*, vol. 19, no. 2, pp. 472–85.

Lisa has been careful to list all the material she has referenced in her essay (though all are not shown here).

5.9 Summary

An essay is another distinctive form of written communication. An essay writer is required to argue, defend or justify a point or view with respect to a particular topic or question. Essays differ from reports both in format and in the style of writing used.

The use of headings within essays is a contentious issue. Some say that headings are inappropriate in essays and interfere with the flow of argument. Others contend that headings provide useful signposts for the reader. The use of headings, appropriate writing styles for essays, how to analyse an essay topic, how to research essay topics and other useful hints for writing essays have been detailed in this chapter. A sample essay has also been included to illustrate the main issues discussed in the chapter.

5.10 Some variations on the formal essay structure

At times you will be asked to present assignments in forms other than 'formal' essays. You should read the instructions for these very carefully and note specifically any deviations from the formal essay format described here. Such variations will relate primarily to the use of headings and subheadings. Terms used by instructors to describe such modified essays may include *critical essays*, *critical discussion*, *comprehensive analysis* or simply *discussion*.

Oral presentations

6 Oral presentations

6.1 Overview

The ability to deliver oral presentations in a competent and confident manner is a skill that is vital for every contemporary business professional. Even the best ideas can be lost if they are not effectively communicated to others.

One important factor that sets oral communication apart from written communication is *immediacy*. Written communication offers authors the opportunity to revise their work continually, until they are satisfied that their message is clear and concise, before delivering the finished work to the reader. The reader can then absorb the message at leisure, reviewing the material as many times as is required to fully understand the author's point of view. In oral communication, the presenter usually has only one chance to deliver the message to the audience and, unless the presentation is recorded, the audience gets only one chance to comprehend the message.

When delivering an oral presentation, it is therefore very important that you use what might be your only chance to convey your message in the most effective manner possible.

Many very useful sources of information are available on how to deliver effective oral presentations. Students should refer to these for detailed information. The guidelines below will provide a useful starting point for developing effective presentations.

6.2 Oral presentations at university

While it is important to read up on how to deliver good oral presentations, this alone will not make you a good presenter. The essential component in developing good oral communication skills is practice. During a student's study at university, many opportunities are provided to practise and develop oral communication skills. This may simply involve participation in informal discussions during tutorial sessions and at residential schools, or it may involve delivering formal presentations that form a component of assessment.

Sometimes students may be asked to prepare oral presentations on tape. The following guidelines will not only assist in the preparation of oral presentations, but will provide an indication of the points that will be considered by those assessing the quality of student presentations.

Oral delivery of any formal presentation involves three main stages:

- preparing the presentation
- delivering the presentation
- handling questions from the audience.

6.3 Preparing the presentation

Preparation is the most important stage in any formal presentation.

The objectives
The first step in preparing a presentation is to decide:

- the purpose of the presentation (i.e. what you wish to achieve)

- who the audience will be.

Purpose of the presentation
The primary purpose of most oral presentations is to entertain, persuade or inform.

Most formal business presentations tend to fall into the latter two categories (i.e. to persuade and/or inform). The objective of a presentation designed primarily to *inform* an audience is to deliver the information in as accurate and efficient a manner as possible. A presentation designed to *persuade* an audience, on the other hand, will seek to influence the beliefs or attitudes of the audience in some way (e.g. to 'sell' a product or idea). The purpose of the presentation must be clearly determined before starting to create the presentation. Having a clear idea of the purpose will assist in deciding on both the content of the presentation and the most effective presentation method.

Audience
The presenter should try to find out as much as possible about the audience before starting to create the presentation. The following questions may assist in analysing the audience:

- What will the audience be expecting from the presentation?

- How much do they already know about the topic of the presentation?

- Will they be receptive or hostile to the information presented in the topic?

- Is the audience composed of technical or non-technical people?

- Are there any sensitive issues (e.g. political or cultural) that should be avoided for this audience?

- How much time does the audience have? (What is the cost of its time?)

- What standard of dress should be adopted for delivery of the presentation?

In summary, your presentation, regardless of the audience, needs to:

(a) be concise, informative and free of technical jargon; and (b) avoid tedious explanations of complex technical issues.

Timing

The presentation should be timed carefully. If it is too short, there is a risk that the opportunity to present your well-researched and -formulated ideas could be forfeited. Overly long presentations are discourteous to following speakers, and listeners are likely to become bored.

6.3.1 Presentation venue

It is important, in the early stages of preparation for the presentation, to learn what you can about the presentation venue. Information on such things as the size of the room and the facilities available will assist in preparing the presentation to best advantage. For example, some presenters like to use computer-based methods as a presentation medium but may discover that the venue does not provide such facilities.

It is also important to arrive at the venue early in order to check that the equipment is functioning correctly and that you have compatible versions of any software you intend to use. Overhead transparencies, which require different preparation and presentation techniques, might then be the only alternative.

6.3.2 Structure of the presentation

Formal oral presentations must be well structured in order to be effective. Like formal written documents, they are made up of:

- an introduction

- a body

- a conclusion.

As the old adage says, 'Tell them what you're going to tell them, tell them, and tell them what you've told them'.

6.3.3 Introduction and conclusion

The main purpose of the introduction is for the speaker to introduce him- or herself (sometimes a session presenter will do this before the speaker begins), to establish a rapport with the audience and to introduce the main points that will be covered in the body of the presentation.

The purpose of the conclusion is to summarise and re-emphasise the main points of the presentation. If the objective of the presentation is to persuade the audience, then the conclusion is the place to reinforce in the minds of the audience exactly what action should be taken. The audience will then leave with that thought uppermost in their minds. The conclusion is a very important component of the presentation and should not be neglected.

Preparation of the introduction and conclusion should normally be left until after the main body of the presentation has been created to ensure that every aspect of the presentation has been addressed. As a general rule, the introduction and conclusion should each occupy approximately 10 percent of the presentation.

6.3.4 Body of the presentation

The body of the presentation should also be structured and presented in a logical sequence. The easiest way to prepare the body of the presentation is as follows:

1 Write down or highlight (you could use an outliner in a word processing program) all of the main points to be covered during the presentation. These will be the major 'signposts' in the presentation. (If presenting in a team, topics may be divided among the team members.)

2 Decide on appropriate sub-topics within each of the main points chosen.

3 The library, or other information sources, can now be used with a clear idea of the material that must be researched in order to complete the body of the presentation.

Using this approach achieves two objectives: first, it imposes a natural structure on the presentation; and second, it helps to ensure the major issues are not overlooked. Some research may be needed before step 1 if the topic of the presentation is unfamiliar to the presenter.

When creating the body of the presentation, it is also worth noting that using simple analogies can often help to convey an idea or message quickly and effectively to the audience — for example, using a well-known organisation or an event that has been discussed in the newspapers recently. It is therefore worth spending time thinking about the best way to convey the message.

6.3.5 Visual aids

Sight plays a major role in the ability to absorb information. Most readers will be familiar with the saying 'A picture is worth a thousand words'. Well-designed visual aids provide a useful complement to most presentations for the following reasons:

■ They can be used to reinforce what is being said.

■ They can help maintain audience interest and concentration.

■ They can be used to illustrate concepts that are difficult to explain verbally.

■ They are a useful prompt for the presenter.

The most common visual aids are created on overhead transparencies and, more recently, using computer packages such as Microsoft PowerPoint. Irrespective of the presentation medium used, visual aids must be well designed; otherwise they can detract from the overall effectiveness of the presentation. The following points should be kept in mind when preparing visual aids:

■ Make sure the slides are not too cluttered; use large fonts (24 point is recommended).

■ Use a mixture of upper- and lower-case letters, and present one major topic per slide.

- Include a maximum of seven points per slide.

- Make sure the slides may be easily read by everyone in the audience.

- Make use of diagrams or graphics where possible, rather than using a lot of text.

- If using diagrams or graphs, keep them simple and uncluttered.

- Use colour if possible, but sparingly and appropriately (no more than 3–4 different colours on the one slide). Choose foreground/background colour combinations that allow any text to be easily read by the audience.

- Ensure that all slides follow a consistent style (i.e. the topic in the same spot on every slide, a similar background on each slide etc.). This makes it easier for the audience to follow.

- Do not use too many slides (no more than one every five minutes).

6.3.6 Audience handouts

Handouts are useful, particularly when the presenter seeks to persuade the audience, both during (to reinforce the information being presented) and after the presentation. Generally, handouts will contain a list of the major points being discussed in the presentation and perhaps a summary of the main message of the presentation. This type of handout should be distributed before the presentation, although some people suggest that this can distract the audience from what you are saying. If the audience is likely to want to take notes about your presentation, then handing out information first is a good idea.

If the presentation requires the review of very detailed or voluminous information, it is usually better to summarise the information verbally during the presentation and to provide more detailed information in handouts for the audience. These handouts should be distributed afterwards in order that the audience is not distracted during the presentation. To draw attention to the handouts, the presenter should mention them at an appropriate point during the presentation.

6.3.7 Practising the presentation

To perform at their very best on the day, sportsmen and -women must practise their skills before the event. Preparing for a formal presentation is no different. Presenters should deliver their presentation at least once (preferably twice), as if they were presenting it to a live audience. Having someone there to provide a critique of the practice presentation is also helpful (this is easier if you are presenting as a member of a team).

Practice is important for a number of reasons:

- It instils confidence in the presenter.

- It will reveal if the presentation will fit into the time allowed (not too long or too short).

- It provides a 'testing ground' for the visual aids (are they too small, too cluttered etc.?).

- If presenting in a team, transitions from one speaker to the next can be practised.

- If you can practise in the room in which the real presentation will take place, you will have the opportunity to familiarise yourself with the equipment to be used.

6.3.8 Planning for contingencies

It is important to plan for possible unexpected events on the day of the presentation. For example, if the presentation time is unexpectedly reduced, which parts could be omitted without interrupting the flow?

Presenters should plan for possible equipment failure. What happens if the computer system that is to be used for the presentation fails two minutes before the presentation is due to start? A possible solution to this problem is to have overhead transparencies prepared as a backup in case this occurs.

The presenter should also try to anticipate possible questions from the audience and prepare answers accordingly. If presenting in a team, it should be decided beforehand whether one person will act as the spokesperson who answers all the questions or whether each team member will address questions on one particular aspect of the presentation.

6.3.9 Just before the presentation

The presenter should aim to arrive at the venue at least 30 minutes before the presentation is due to start. This will allow plenty of time to ensure that the seating arrangements for the audience are appropriate and the equipment is functioning correctly. It will also provide some time to overcome any anxiety experienced by the presenter.

6.3.10 Equipment

The presenter should ensure that any equipment required for the presentation is set up and functioning correctly and that instructions for operating the equipment and lighting in the room are understood. This applies in particular to complicated computer and audiovisual equipment. Last-minute equipment failure can be a disaster for the presenter who has not anticipated it.

6.3.11 Anxiety

Most people experience a degree of anxiety when faced with making a public presentation. This is natural, but uncontrolled nervousness can detract from an otherwise good presentation. At this point, presenters should already have addressed the first two steps towards controlling anxiety — *preparation* and *practice*. Being prepared, having a good knowledge of the content of the presentation, and knowing that it will work because it has been practised will instil confidence and help to reduce nervousness.

If you still feel nervous, take a few deep breaths (try not to hyperventilate). This will help to release tension. Another way to relax is to gradually tense every muscle in the body, starting from the feet through to the neck, arms and hands, then slowly release the tension and take a deep breath. Doing this once or twice should help you feel more relaxed.

6.4 Delivering the presentation

6.4.1 Delivery speed

When delivering presentations it is important to avoid speaking too quickly. Generally, the speed of the presentation should be rather slower than the speed of normal conversation. You should slow down if speaking too quickly or jumbling words, or if the audience appears not to be following your argument because the topics are being covered too quickly.

6.4.2 Gestures

Natural gestures will add a further dimension to presentations. Anxiety can sometimes cause gestures to be a little stiff and unnatural. However, as the presentation progresses and the presenter feels more comfortable, it is often easier to use gestures more naturally. Whether gestures are used at all is entirely optional. Actions you should definitely avoid include folding your arms, putting your hands in your pockets or nervously wringing your hands. These gestures can be very distracting for the audience.

6.4.3 Audience rapport

During the presentation it is very important for each member of the audience to feel as though he or she is being addressed personally. One method that will help establish a rapport with the audience is to maintain eye contact. If presenting to a small group, try to focus on each person for approximately 1–3 seconds before moving on to the next. If presenting to a large group of people, maintaining eye contact with each individual becomes very difficult. In this case, select small groups of people in the audience and focus on someone within each group before moving on to the next group. In this way, despite the distance between speaker and audience, each member of the audience will still feel as though he or she is being addressed personally.

Focusing just above the back row and sweeping your eyes across a large auditorium is another technique that will help to achieve this result.

6.4.4 Reading the speech

In some cases, reading a speech in its entirety is necessary; however, in general reading a presentation is not acceptable. When a speech is read, maintaining eye contact with the audience becomes much more difficult; it is therefore much harder to maintain the audience's attention.

Rote-learning a speech is also not a good practice to adopt. This tends to make the speech sound stilted. It is also very easy to experience memory lapses due to nervousness — which can lead to very uncomfortable silences.

Using notes or presentation slides as prompts is a much better approach to adopt.

6.4.5 Stance during the speech

The presenter should not slouch or stand too stiffly. Best is a relaxed, upright posture, with the weight evenly distributed to both legs. If available, a lectern should be used. A lectern provides a place for your presentation notes, as well as somewhere to rest your hands (and behind which to hide your shaking knees!).

When delivering a presentation, it is important to try not to stand with feet fixed in one spot. Continually pacing backwards and forwards is not acceptable either, since it can be distracting for the audience. An occasional step towards the audience can help to emphasise a point and help to maintain attention. Moving about a little during the presentation can also help to relieve tension.

6.4.6 Humour

Humour can be useful in establishing and maintaining a rapport with the audience, but humour should be used wisely, otherwise you risk alienating your listeners. Take care to:

- avoid humour that could potentially offend any member of the audience;
- try to link humour to the speaker, topic, audience or occasion; and
- avoid using humour unless confident that it will be well received by the audience and will add to the presentation.

6.4.7 Nervousness

If you are nervous during the presentation, avoid actions such as holding up pieces of paper, which will communicate this nervousness to the audience. Ensure some water is available, because if your mouth becomes dry you may start coughing and find it difficult to project your voice well.

6.4.8 Annoying habits

Try to avoid 'ums', 'ahs' and 'errs' in your address, along with actions such as continually tapping your feet, or drumming a pointer or pen on the lectern. These often subconscious manifestations of nervousness can become most annoying for the audience and risk distracting attention from your message.

6.4.9 Presenting in teams

Presenting in teams is, on one hand, less stressful for each individual team member because others are there to share the responsibility. On the other hand, if the team does not work well together during the presentation this can be very distracting for the audience.

Co-presenters should carry out the following steps to ensure they work well together and that the presentation flows smoothly from beginning to end:

- Decide before the presentation which presenters will deliver which parts of the presentation.

- Practise the presentation as a team before delivering it on the day.

- Decide before the presentation how questions will be answered and which team members will be responsible for answering questions after the presentation.

- Introduce each team member during the introduction, and tell the audience which aspect of the topic each speaker will address.

- As the presentation passes from one speaker to the next, the former should introduce the latter and briefly remind the audience which aspect that speaker will address.

It is also important that, if presenting in a team, *all* team members participate.

6.5 Handling questions from the audience

In most cases, time will be allocated after the presentation for questions from the audience. The person answering audience questions should:

- clarify and summarise questions that are verbose

- restate all questions to ensure everyone in the audience has heard them (unless the group is very small)

- if unable to answer a particular question, be honest and say so. Also indicate that an answer will be found and relayed to the person asking the question.

6.6 Summary

Earlier chapters focused on written communication techniques. It is essential for contemporary business professionals not only to have good written communication skills, but also to develop good oral presentation skills.

Oral presentation is not an easy skill to master, and presenters usually have only one opportunity to deliver their message effectively. Therefore, it is vital that before the presentation the speaker has done sufficient preparation and planning to ensure that the content, visual aids, delivery speed and other key components of the presentation are appropriate for the intended audience.

In order to prepare and deliver effective oral presentations, students should have:

- decided on the purpose of the presentation

- analysed the prospective audience

- decided on the timing of the presentation

- prepared the presentation venue
- structured the presentation appropriately
- prepared effective visual aids
- prepared audience handouts
- practised the presentation.

They should also be confident in:

- handling presentation equipment
- planning for contingencies
- dealing with pre-presentation anxiety
- presenting at an appropriate speed
- gesturing during the presentation
- developing a rapport with the audience
- knowing when and when not to *read* a speech
- knowing how to stand during the speech
- knowing how humour should be used
- overcoming nervousness
- eliminating annoying habits during the presentation
- presenting in teams
- handling questions from the audience.

These issues have been discussed in detail, and hints and techniques for delivering better presentations have been provided in this chapter.

6.7 Alternatives to oral presentations for distance education students

In some Business courses, distance students (including on-line students) will be required to submit 'oral' presentations electronically or in the form of an audiotape or videotape. For these types of presentations students should apply the same principles and preparation guidelines as outlined here. In these situations, students should attempt to simulate as far as possible a face-to-face presentation, and audiovisual aids may be appropriately integrated into such presentations. It is also important to adhere strictly to any time length guidelines imposed by the instructor. Every attempt should be made to maximise the reproduction quality of such presentations.

Examination techniques

7 Examination techniques[4]

7.1 Introduction

There are a number of ways in which a student can successfully study for and sit an examination. Not all techniques work for everyone. You will need to choose the techniques that best suit you. Most important is to decide how best to approach the examination period and to formulate a plan of action to enable you to perform at your best. Following is a list of suggestions, in terms of exam technique, that you may adapt to an individualised plan of attack.

7.2 General hints

7.2.1 When to start studying

Do not leave everything to the last minute. This is a very common and important piece of advice with regard to exams, but it is often easier said than done. Learning theory suggests that a steady and routine approach to learning is far better than a period of mad cramming at the end. Furthermore, reliance on short-term memory is illusory: tests have shown that retention rates can be measured in hours, whereas long-term memory becomes more reliable with every reinforcement. Therefore, it makes sense to plan to address each of your courses regularly and consistently throughout the semester, and to keep to this plan as far as is practicable.

7.2.2 Revision

The following hints may help you to better plan and prepare for your examinations.

- Revise with a purpose. Find out the exam format; take note of the objectives of the unit, as well as of the individual modules; look at past exam papers for the subject (often available in the library); and review your assignments and the instructor's comments. This information will provide a guide to the likely focus of the exam. Then you will be able to structure your revision around the most important areas, rather than trying to cover everything in the same depth. If, because of extensive revision of subject material, there are no prior exam papers to rely on (or if the whole course is new), then you should ask the instructor for sample questions.

- Find out the exact meaning of terms such as *analyse*, *comment*, *compare*, *contrast*, *describe*, *relate*, *define*, *distinguish*, *discuss*, *explain*, *illustrate*, *justify*, *list*, *outline*, *state* and *summarise* (see the glossary on page 93 for definitions of key instructions).

- Allow adequate time for revision. If you have not left yourself enough time to cover the material, last-minute cramming may serve only to leave you painfully aware of how much you do not know — and in a state of panic. Once you

---

4. This section was originally developed by Mr Frank Jarvis (now deceased); his input is gratefully acknowledged.

know your exam timetable, it is a good idea to formulate a study timetable so that you can use your time to greatest advantage.

- Revision should include a variety of activities. Rather than just attempting to commit volumes of information to memory, try to do things a little differently. Attempt past exam questions under exam conditions, or write your own exam questions — you might be surprised by how close you come to the actual exam questions. Produce summaries of summaries so that a word or phrase might trigger your memory; organise regular short study sessions with other students.

- Take regular breaks and allow for adequate rest. It is good to have a balanced approach; try to take some time out for exercise and to eat well. This can break the monotony of study, as well as improving your physical and mental state.

7.3 Pre-examination planning

- Make sure you know where and when the exam is to take place. It is essential that you leave yourself plenty of time to get to the exam venue, particularly when some travel is involved. You should also take into account problems of parking, if this applies.

- Check that you have all the necessary equipment. Writing materials, erasers, correction fluid, highlighting pens, straight edges, calculators and anything else that is permitted in the exam room should be in good working order (pens run dry, pencils snap, batteries run out etc.).

- Check what (if any) written/printed materials are permitted in the exam room, and make sure you have these with you. You should also determine in advance if any qualifications apply (use of highlighter pens, marginal notes and/or Post-it labels may be forbidden).

7.3.1 Perusal time

- Use your perusal time wisely. The first thing you must do is read the instructions on the cover page carefully: there have been instances of students failing to notice that they were required to answer only a set number of questions and not the entire paper. Then read the exam script carefully.

- If you are given a choice of questions, use this time to decide which ones you will answer and in what order.

- Work out the time you have to answer each question. (Do this before the exam if you know the format and weightings.) Use the marks allocated to the question as a guide to how much time you will need to answer the question. When working out the timing, leave sufficient time at the end of the exam to review your answers.

- If permitted, use perusal time to make brief notes about the questions on the exam paper, but not in the exam booklet.

7.3.2 After the examination begins

■ ***Try not to panic.*** Take a deep breath and begin on a question or questions you feel confident about answering. Try doing the question(s) you feel least confident about second, so that you have them out of the way early on. An alternative approach is to answer short questions first.

■ Clearly mark the question number or part of the exam that you are answering. Begin each question on a new page.

■ Watch your time carefully. Try not to go over time on any questions, as you may end up with very little time left for the last one or with no time to review your answers. The number of marks allocated will normally be a guide to how long you should spend on the question/part-question. Here are two rules of thumb:

- Allow approximately 30 percent of the time you have allocated to each question for thinking and organising how you will answer the question.

- Periodically check the time you have left, but remember that alarm watches are discouraged since they disturb others' concentration.

■ Do not leave the examination room early: any time you have left over is much better employed reviewing what you have written (see below).

■ Make sure that you answer each of the questions to the extent expected by the examiner. What is expected in your answer should be clear from the body of the question. Refer to Section 7.4 for hints on what the examiner might be expecting for specific types of questions.

■ Make sure you answer the question the examiner has actually asked and make sure you have answered all of the question, not just part of it (refer to the glossary of key instructions on page 93).

■ Finally, take a few minutes to check your answers carefully for any silly errors. Return to questions you might have left and attempt them again. Ensure you have entered your name on every exam booklet and have ticked the questions answered in each booklet.

7.4 Content and style of questions

This section gives some useful examples of the styles of question that might be experienced when sitting for an examination. For each style of question, guidelines to the form that appropriate answers should take are offered.

7.4.1 Subject matter limited

Some questions may be worded in a way that limits the subject matter. Answers to these questions should be worded so that they keep strictly to the topic. For example, questions might include the words:

- 'using ... as an example ...'
- 'with respect to ...'
- 'referring to ...'

7.4.2 Scope limited

Some questions may be worded so that the scope is limited. For example:

- 'List four ...'
- 'Evaluate the major impact of ...'
- 'List the main advantages and disadvantages ...'

Answers should once again be restricted to the question's parameters.

7.4.3 Combined subject and scope limited

Some questions may combine scope and subject matter limitation. For example:

- 'Using no more than two examples ...'

Watch for key words in questions that will guide you in how to answer (see the glossary on p. 93). For example:

- 'What ...' usually indicates that the examiner is testing the **scope** of your knowledge.
- 'Why ...' or 'How ...' is testing your **analytical** skills.
- 'Differentiate ...' or 'Compare ...' invites you to present two sides of an argument.

7.4.4 Multiple-choice questions

Be sure to read the question and choices very carefully. If unsure of an answer, use a process of elimination, but do not spend too long on a question that you find difficult — return to it at the end.

7.4.5 Short-answer questions

This type of question is designed to elicit brief (one-sentence or, at the most, one-paragraph) responses.

These are distinguished by key instructions such as:

- 'briefly state/discuss, etc ...'
- 'write short notes on ...'
- 'explain/expand the following [term/acronym] ...'
- 'outline ...'

7.4.6 Point-by-point questions

This type of question is designed to elicit multi-line answers, sometimes in a structured form (e.g. 'show in a table'). These are distinguished by key instructions such as:

- 'enumerate ...'
- 'list ...'
- 'tabulate ...'

Be careful to distinguish between key instructions such as 'enumerate' and 'list': the former may imply some form of ranking and should elicit a numbered list (1 being the most important); the latter can be answered in dot-point form.

Some key instructions, such as 'compare' and 'contrast', also lend themselves to answers in tabular form. Be sure to line up your answers logically, as shown below:

Object A	Object B
1	1
2	2
3	3

The use of boxes allows you (and the marker) to test the logic of your answer.

7.4.7 Essay-style questions

These questions are designed to elicit multi-paragraph, structured answers, depending on the keyword used. Formulate your answers with care. Because of the time constraints, students are often concerned simply to regurgitate as much information as possible in exams. However, even in an exam it is important to follow the usual essay structure of introduction, body and conclusion and to organise your main points in a logical manner. This takes less time than you might think and is actually useful in ensuring that you remember to include important points. It also makes your exam easier to read and better demonstrates your understanding of the subject matter (see Chapter 5 for more information about how to approach and write an essay).

Essay-style questions are distinguished by key instructions such as:

- 'discuss ...'
- 'evaluate ...'
- 'debate ...'
- 'analyse ...'
- 'examine critically ...'

7.4.8 Hybrid questions

This type of question is designed to elicit answers that contain an essay component and point-by-point answers. They are distinguished by key instructions such as:

- 'list, giving reasons ...'
- 'draw a model and discuss the major components of the model ...'

7.4.9 Case studies

These are distinguished by a short piece of text followed by questions relating to that text. These questions may be of any type.

Remember to read the text *carefully*. Use underlining or a highlighter pen to identify key words or phrases (see Chapter 4 for more information about how to answer a case study question).

7.4.10 Other types of questions

You may also encounter other forms of questions in examinations. For example, you may be given key instructions such as:

- 'illustrate using diagrams ...'
- 'sketch ...'

These types of questions are designed to elicit very specific forms of non-text answers. Be sure either to label the components of a diagram or to annotate them and enter the text below the diagram.

7.5 Do's and don'ts when answering examination questions

Do's

- Remember that the people marking your script are only human: try at all times to assist them in evaluating your answers.

- Write legibly (print if your writing is difficult to read). Remember that the marker is not obliged to interpret the answer in your favour.

- Read what you have written. If *you* are unable to make sense of your answer, then the marker will be in the same position.

- Skip to the next question if your mind goes blank. Better still, take a brief rest before skipping.

- Read the question carefully and answer the question that is put to you, *not* the question you would like to have been put. This is a common failing among students who wish to display their knowledge but don't know the specific answer required.

- Use subheadings in a long answer. As well as showing a logical approach, this makes your answer more readable.

- Leave a blank line after subheadings.

- Leave plenty of space between answers to questions. During the review process you might find that you want to write more and this saves messy bubbles and pointers directing the marker to your afterthoughts.

- Start each question on a new page and number the question correctly.

- Rewrite the answer neatly if too many corrections are needed.

- Use the left page for rough work only. The marker will usually ignore the left page altogether.

Don'ts

- Don't repeat yourself (or the question). Some students write out the question in full. This is a waste of time.

- Don't spend more than your calculated time on any question. If there is time left over you can always return to it.

- Avoid waffle. The point made earlier about spending a significant proportion of your time in planning is reinforced here: a well-planned answer should contain no redundant information.

- Never use words you cannot spell. This is particularly true for words that relate specifically to your discipline area, since it will create a poor impression if you misspell terms you are expected to be familiar with.

- Don't write notes to the examiner/marker, particularly rude or facetious ones.

- A new question should not be started at the bottom of a page. The marker might miss an important continuity.

- Never cram a diagram into the last few lines on a page, particularly if you are using an annotated diagram: the marker will have to keep turning the page back and forth.

- Don't write in red on the answer booklet. Since red is the colour generally used by markers, exam answers written in red can cause confusion.

- Never start a new question in the middle of a line. The marker might well miss it or assume that your text refers to the previous question.

7.6 Summary

The examination period can be a very stressful time for students. However, much of the stress associated with exams can be reduced by thorough preparation and by making the most effective use of the time spent during the exam. This chapter has provided some suggestions on how to study and when to start studying for exams.

Some students run out of time during examinations and are forced to leave entire questions unanswered. This usually results in a poor overall performance. Students who make effective use of perusal time and working time in examinations usually perform well. This chapter has provided useful hints to help students develop effective examination techniques.

The way a question is worded will normally give a clear indication of the examiner's expectation in terms of the format and content of the answer. Examples of various types of questions and the answers expected have also been provided.

The chapter ended with a list of do's and don'ts that should help enhance a student's chances of success in an examination.

Glossary of key instructions

Analyse	Show the essence of something by breaking it down into component parts, examining each part in detail and showing how the parts fit together.
Argue	Present the case for and/or against a particular proposition.
Compare	Look for similarities between propositions or objects.
Contrast	Look for differences between propositions or objects.
Criticise	Give your judgement, backed by a discussion of the evidence, on the merit of theories or opinions or the truth of 'facts'.
Debate	Argue from two or more viewpoints.
Define	Set down the precise meaning of a word or phrase. Show that the distinctions implied in the definition are necessary.
Describe	Give a detailed or graphic account of.
Differentiate	As for 'distinguish'.
Discuss	Investigate or examine by argument; sift and debate, giving reasons for and against.
Distinguish	Find differences between two or more apparently different propositions, ideas or objects.
Draw	1. Make a diagram of (an object) 2. Argue for or against a proposition, producing 'a/some conclusion(s) from it'.
Enumerate	List or specify and describe in a structured manner, and prioritise.
Evaluate	Make an appraisal of the worth of something, in the light of its apparent truth or utility; include your personal opinion.
Examine	Present in depth and investigate the implications of.
Expand	Give the full meaning of an acronym or abbreviation.
Explain	Make plain; interpret and account for in detail.
Illustrate	Explain and make clear using concrete written examples or a figure or diagram.
Interpret	Bring out the meaning of, and make clear and explicit, usually also giving your own judgement.

Justify   Show adequate grounds for decisions or conclusions.

Outline   Give the main features or general principles of a subject, omitting minor details, and emphasising structure and relationship.

Prove   1. Demonstrate the truth or falsity by presenting evidence.
                 2. Provide a mathematical/logical proof.

Relate   Narrate/show how things are connected to each other and to what extent they are alike or affect each other.

Review   Make a survey of, examining the subject critically.

Sketch   Draw a freehand picture.

State   Specify fully and clearly.

Summarise   Give a concise account of the chief points or substance of a matter, omitting details and examples.

Trace   Identify and describe the development or history of a topic from some point or origin.

(Adapted from Queensland University of Technology 1988, *The written assignment*, Brisbane, p. 27)

List of references

Deakin University 1993, *Faculty of Arts style guide*, Geelong.

Elms, J 1993, *Essay assignments: a user friendly guide*, University of Southern Queensland Student Association, Toowoomba.

Kashani, K 1992, *Managing global marketing*, PWS Kent, USA.

Lovell, DW & Moore, RD 1993, *Essay writing and style guide for politics and the social sciences*, Australian Political Studies Association, Canberra.

Lovelock, CH 1991, *Services marketing*, 2nd edn, Prentice Hall, Englewood Cliffs, New Jersey.

Mandel, S 1993, *Effective presentation skills: a practical guide for better speaking*, Career Builders, Brisbane.

Perry, C (n.d.), *A structured approach to presenting PhD theses: notes for candidates and their supervisors*, unpublished paper, School of Marketing, Advertising and Public Relations, Queensland University of Technology.

Style manual for authors, editors and printers 2002, 6th edn, John Wiley & Sons, Brisbane.

University of Queensland, Gatton College 1994, *A guide to preparing and presenting written assignments*, eds J. Summers and C. Pedersen, Department of Business Studies, Gatton.

Queensland University of Technology 1989, *The written assignment*, Brisbane.

University of Southern Queensland 1994, *Communications,* Distance Education Centre, Toowoomba.

Wrigley, J & McLean, P 1990, *Australian business communication*, 2nd edn, Longman Cheshire, Melbourne.

Index

index